The Faces of Feminism

Why Do We Fear Feminism?

Maria M. Bermudez

Rogue Books
Bedazzled Ink Publishing Company • Fairfield, California

978-1-939562-19-7 paperback
978-1-939562-20-3 ebook

Cover Design
by
C.A. Casey

Rogue Books
a division of
Bedazzled Ink Publishing Company
Fairfield, California
http://www.bedazzledink.com/

To M.L.S. and E.A.G.
Thank you for your love and support

Contents

Impacts of Feminism on Society

[The reason why women have still not achieved equality with men is] . . . because women have been taught always to work for something else than their own personal freedom; and the hardest thing in the world is to organize women for the one purpose of securing their political liberty and political equality.
—Susan B. Anthony[1]

1 Paulson, Ross Evans. (1997) *Liberty, Equality and Justice: Civil Rights, Women's Rights, and the Regulation of Business, 1865-1932.* Duke University Press. p 95.

INTRODUCTION

I first began to toy with the idea of writing this book several years ago after realizing that a large population of the students I was teaching had absolutely no concept of what feminism was about, and their only point of reference was what the media had to say concerning a bunch of butch bra-burning viragos.

More than once has my jaw dropped in total astonishment at what my students—both male and female—have come up with when confronted with the question, "What is Feminism?" Indeed, the question is not easy to answer, but even the reaction to, "Would you consider yourself a feminist?" was surprising, especially by the females. Answers to this question have ranged from, "Heck no! I'm not a lesbian!" to the response of a young Venezuelan male who stated that the world needed more feminists. His vehement comment left everyone in the classroom puzzled and, when I probed further, he stated that the world needed more feminists because the women of today are not as feminine as they had been fifty years ago. According to him, the women of today needed more "feminization" and needed to grasp the concept of feminism to be truly feminine. I will not even try to describe the ensuing ruckus his comments triggered.

I have been teaching for over twenty years and have taught in different countries around the world

(Zimbabwe, USA, Spain, Venezuela, Canada, and the UK). Invariably, when I ask my students to give their opinions concerning feminism (unless they are actively involved with feminist courses/issues one way or another) the general concept of feminism is totally negative. This is because the popular media has disseminated a series of myths that have been assimilated by the general population as scientifically proven facts. In fact, I would go as far as to say that the popular media has done more damage than good to one half of the population: women.

Because of the popular media's insistence of discrediting and placing half the population in a subordinate position, and elevating the other half—the male half of the population—many women have come to believe that this is the rightful place of men. Unfortunately, these women have allowed themselves—and their offspring—to be brainwashed into believing that men are superior, and women are inferior and that the word "feminism" is a curse. At the same time, these brainwashed women who follow blindly whatever the media suggests, knowingly or unknowingly set about to discredit the work of other women who have fought to claim their rights as human beings. Many anti-feminist women do not realize that they hold a job today thanks to the unrelenting work of feminists. Anti-feminist women have constitutional rights thanks to the indefatigable work of feminists; anti-feminist women have a standing as a member of society thanks to the obstinacy and steadfastness of feminists; anti-feminist women have an education thanks to the persistent work of feminists.

What exactly is feminism and why does it draw so much media attention? Why do people talk about it so much? Why do people love and hate it to the passionate degree of heated debates?

Perhaps it is because it strikes at the core of a major social construct: gender. Gender is an important social construct in every single society around the world, and once constructs become the target of scrutiny and questioning, power, politics, economics, and a thousand other related constructs also come into question. Ultimately, the greatest fear is that there may be a shift, or worse, a displacement of the overall notion that surrounds that construct.

By definition, gender separates the human species into male and female and, as such, society has attributed roles to both genders, relying solely on social constructs and biological factors. The fact that gender has been a topic of major importance throughout history is without question, as can be seen from writings—popular fiction, poetry, and in scholarly papers—and works of art as well as other subjects. In short, the "woman question" has always been there, influencing every area of society from politics (should women have the right to vote?) to traditional family values (should women work?) to every other field one cares to mention.

So, what exactly is feminism?

According to the Merriam-Webster Online dictionary, feminism is: "1) the theory of the political, economic, and social equality of the sexes and 2) [feminism is the] organized activity on behalf of women's rights and interests."[2]

According to the WordNet lexical database for

English from Princeton University, feminism is "a doctrine that advocates equal rights for women."[3]

A slightly longer and more inclusive definition of feminism can be obtained from Cheris Kramarae and Paula A. Treichler, who, in their book, *A Feminist Dictionary* (1985), devote three pages to different definitions expounded by different women writers, beginning with a short summary of the three basic positions of feminism during the years between 1400 and 1789. They quote Millicent Garrett Fawcett (1878) for having said that feminism has as its goal to give every woman "the opportunity of becoming the best that her natural faculties make her capable of."[4]

Kramarae and Treichler go through history, quoting different women and their definitions of feminism. They quote Teresa Billington-Grieg (1911) as stating that "Feminism may be defined as a movement seeking the reorganization of the world upon a basis of sex-equality in all human relations; a movement which would reject every differentiation between individuals upon the ground of sex, would abolish all sex privileges and sex burdens, and would strive to set up the recognition of the common humanity of woman and man as the foundation of law and custom."[5]

The authors culminate with the year 1983 (just before the manuscript was sent to the press). They quote Rebecca Lewin (1983), who states that "feminism is a theory that calls for women's attainment of social, economic, and political rights and opportunities equal

---

3 WordNet lexical database for English from Princeton University. In http://wordnet.princeton.edu/

4 Kramarae, Cheris, and Treichler, Paula A., (1985) *A Feminist Dictionary.* Pandora Press. P.158.

5 Ibid.

to those possessed by men. Feminism is also a model for a social state—an ideal, or a desired standard of perfection not yet attained in the world."[6]

There are as many definitions of feminism as there are feminists and scholars attempting a definition. The overall consensus within all those definitions of the role of feminism is the deconstruction of these gender delineations or categories. Whichever way one sees it, at the heart of the argument is the realization that there is no real fundamental definition of feminism.

Feminism is a political, social, economic, educational, etc., belief that all human beings should be valued in her/his own right. Because women have been constantly underrated, subordinated, and subjugated, the primary role of feminism is to place a stronger emphasis on the "woman issue" by revising all those gender constructs that placed women in such a predicament in the first place. This means reevaluating the meaning of history, psychology, anthropology, politics, literature, economics, and so on, and rethinking all these disciplines in the light of the idea that women have, for the most part, been invisible. Feminist ideology states that women are not invisible anymore.

By definition, then, a feminist is someone who actively deconstructs the meanings of gender as created by society. In other words, when a person—either male or female—advocates for the equal right to university education for women (to use one example) that person has actively deconstructed the social premise that only men are allowed further education; and by the same token, that person has also actively deconstructed the social premise that

6 Ibid. p. 160.

only men are allowed to vie for a job that permits him to exercise within that field of acquired knowledge. By advocating openly, this person has taken privilege from one gender and re-assigned it to both genders; by advocating openly, this person has eliminated subjugation and subordination as social constructs from the definition of gender.

This very simple example leaves a lot to be desired, but it is a starting point. Of course, social constructs run along other lines that bring other issues into the equation—for example, ethnic background, education, age, physical ability/mobility, class, etc.—that make the deconstruction issue more challenging for feminists. Because of this, feminism is a movement that involves political, educational, social, religious, cultural, etc., values and theories. Feminism has permeated every sphere of life because of the simple fact that women are in every single sphere of life, and as long as there are women involved, or the possibility that women could, would, and should be involved, then feminism will definitely have something to say.

We can safely conclude that:

- Feminism is a movement and a revolution . . .
- Feminism is a stance and it is a practice . . .
- Feminism is a philosophy and it is a science . . .
- Feminism is activism and it is academia . . .
- Feminism is diverse and it is focused . . .
- Feminism can be mass-oriented and it can be individual-oriented . . .
- Feminism encompasses rights without boundaries, restrictions, or biases for everyone in our societies regardless of color, ethnic background, creed, socio-economic background, gender, or sexual orientation . . .

Feminism would like to see the gender gap disappear to be replaced by the true equality that could feasibly exist between the genders . . .

Because of this, feminists have branched out into different groups and have taken on many interests earning a variety of tags—to name just a few because the list is extensive:

Academic feminist
Anti-porn feminist
Biblical feminist
Career feminist
Contemporary feminist
Cultural feminist
Domestic feminist
Equality feminist
Historical feminist
Lesbian feminist
Liberal feminist
Male feminist
Marxist feminist

Political feminist
Pro feminist
Pro-sex feminist
Radical feminist
Reform feminist
Scholarly feminist
Socialist feminist
Ultra feminist
Women of Color feminist
Young feminist
Intergenerational feminist

Having said all of the above, the intent of this short book is not to define, confine, or critique. Rather, the intent is to give an impartial look (as far as it is humanly possibly) at a topic that has created waves in our society. It is a book intended for the purpose of instructing at an academic level, and a book that gives the basics of a topic that has been misinterpreted and misjudged because of media prejudice and misunderstanding. In short, it is a book that aspires to give the reader an introductory and, hopefully, unbiased look at feminism. Hopefully, too, this book will pique and further the reader's interest in the topic.

FIRST WAVE FEMINISM

Origins

There is not an exact date that can be pinpointed as *the* date when women began to think about themselves and their situation as women. Although today we use The Declaration of Sentiments[7] as the milestone marking the beginnings of the women's movement, evidence shows that women had been troubled with issues concerning their welfare dating back several centuries.

History is such that a lot of information has been left out, especially when it concerns women. This is because history has been recorded from a very narrow point of view making the female presence in history, for the most part, invisible. We know for a fact that there were rulers (e.g. Wu Zetian and Cleopatra) and queens (e.g. Elizabeth I and Nefertiti), as well as scientists, poets, artists, and many others, too numerous to mention, all of whom we consider celebrities and who stood out for their courage and intellect. However, the times and the societies in which they lived were such that they could not take a stand in order to improve the status of other women.

The question as to when women began to question their status, or lack of, within society still remains a mystery. Women, being part of a society, naturally are subject to influences from every sphere of life. What events led to women wanting to raise

7 See appendix 1 for a transcript of the Declaration.

their consciousness? What happened socially, economically, or historically? These are questions that have no single concrete answer. Several historical events happened in isolation and/or in unison, which led to social changes and upheavals. Some theorists argue that the women's movement originated in the works of Sappho[8], the Greek poetess.

Sappho's work is all that remains—from that ancient world that only male history has recorded—to acknowledge the existence of females. Subsequently, her works are invaluable because she shines some light into the times and lives of women of that era that otherwise would have remained obscured and lost in time. At the same time, Sappho portrays herself as a non-conformist in her society: she dared say "no" to men and also dared speak against the tyranny of her society. Although she was married and enjoyed male company, her homoerotic poetry is of great significance. However, judging from the lack of condemnation from such poetry, we can cautiously surmise that perhaps love between women was not as harshly viewed then as it is now in our modern societies. Hence, for us, now, it is Sappho's voice, a woman's voice, isolated, which, in a few fragments that barely add up to 650 lines, speaks of love, anguish, desire, longing, and suffering.

Little is known of Sappho, but it is known that she was an aristocrat and, as such, could devote herself to whatever she wanted to. Sappho chose to devote herself to the Muses and became what could be termed "the headmistress" of a "school" for young girls. These girls followed Sappho's teaching guidance

8 See appendix 2 for short biography.

concerning the arts, poetry, music, special graces, and worshipping goddesses, specifically the Goddess Aphrodite.

It is due to this scant but powerful evidence that researchers assume that Sappho laid the foundation to the beginnings of the women's movement.

Still, other theorists believe that female consciousness arose during the Renaissance, with female French writers like Christine de Pizan and her book, *The Book of the City of Women* (1405), in which she basically talks about the need for women to build a city apart from men, a city where they will not be "attacked and slandered by men."[9]

Still other theorists believe that women's consciousness arose from the decline of domestic production in the nineteenth century, that is, with the advent of the Industrial Revolution. The Industrial Revolution led to a rapid change in urbanization where small family units were replaced by factory work, and women suddenly found themselves employed in the most menial tasks or at home.

Most theorists, however, concur that women became inspired out of the intellectual, political, and social happenings of the eighteenth century, both in the United States and Europe. This century marks an historical milestone because it was during this era that many thinkers began to reject the omnipresence of the Church, and God was, suddenly, not the source of all knowledge. Thinkers flourished, and, with them, a whole plethora of ideas evolved whereby *truth* about life could only be found by the free exercise of reason

9 Boles, Janet K., and Hoeveler, Diane Long (eds.). 1996. *From the Goddess to the Glass Ceiling: a Dictionary of Feminism.* Madison Books, Maryland. p. 1

and logic. In their quest for finding out reason, logic, truth, rationality, and human perfectibility these thinkers became preoccupied with analyzing events and facts surrounding man, their existing society, and finally woman. Such questions as to whether woman was inferior to man, what roles she should assume in society, whether she was rational or emotional, and so forth, became important. Reason and logic replaced faith, miracles, and blind religious dogma. This was the Age of the Enlightenment.

Briefly, this movement was influenced by the works of Galileo, Pascal, Leibniz, and a number of other philosophers, among them Sir Isaac Newton who later on combined proof with observation to give verifiable results. The Age of Enlightenment set the tone for thinkers like Voltaire and Rousseau to openly attack existing institutions including the Church and the State. Objective truth led to the questioning of the relationship between being and perception. Hume and Berkley devoted much time to this exploration, and so would Kant in his own philosophy. There was a focus on every aspect of life, not just the Church. With respect to the Law, rules were expounded as separate from behavior and experience, and it was postulated that the rights of individuals had nothing to do with ancient traditions. It was in this period that individual liberty was put forth as a fundamental right of man. Hence, the Enlightenment proposed the notions that property, rationality, and liberty were lawful rights of every individual—notions that are still upheld as the basis of most political philosophies today. The idea of rationality as a main force in governments became the basis of the American Declaration of Independence and the ensuing American Constitution in 1787, as well as that of the French Revolution and the Polish Revolution of 1791.

It was an age when everybody was allowed their opinion and, needless to say, women added themselves to the growing list of philosophers, although in far less numbers.[10] Although few women philosophers remain recorded or even known today, such names as Mary Astel, Lady Mary Shepherd, Mary Wollstonecraft, among others, had a social impact and left the foundations of inspiration and encouragement to others like Flora Tristan, Frances Wright, the Grimké sisters, and many others who readily followed in their footsteps. A movement began, slow at first, an undercurrent of only a few isolated voices clamoring for their rights. It was not anything visible or tangible, and only a few historical records remain to show that a storm was brewing, a storm that would culminate in the emergence of the women's movement.

With this insidious and gradual change in consciousness and thought spanning several centuries, it is no wonder that the exact time and place for the emergence of the women's movement has not been pinpointed. Suffice it to say that women's consciousness arose because women realized that they were marginalized, often attacked, and minimized in comparison to men, and many other reasons which suddenly became important for them to change. Feminism became a way of challenging the relationships between men and women and, at the same time, challenging the laws, values, and social conventions that kept women as second-class

---

10 See appendix 3 for short list of notable women philosophers.

citizens. In essence, feminism challenged division of labor and all that made men a dominating force in every sphere of life—government, sports, arts, work, politics.

It would be interesting to have a specific date to mark when feminism began, but historians and researchers are too well aware of how little documentation there is left that records anything concerning women. The reason may be two-fold. First, historical records have, for the most part, recorded the life, times, and work of men. Men of yore did not record—through neglect, carelessness, or unimportance—the lives of women unless, somehow, that record pertained to them. And, secondly, throughout history, humanity has excelled in conquering others, spiritually and otherwise and, in the process, robbing, pilfering, burning, destroying. Added to that is the censoring of close-minded scholars, religious leaders, and power figures who, deliberately and otherwise, have totally eradicated the history of the people conquered. Many historical records have been lost and the chances of finding historical records pertaining to women have been further reduced.

A point in question is the despicable way in which many of Sappho's poems came to light. Late in the nineteenth century, several documents were found in excavations in the Nile Valley and in Egyptian refuse heaps. In one refuse heap, some of these papyruses so carelessly discarded contained Sappho's works. Several other papyruses were found in sealed coffins used as wrappings and stuffing of animals and mummies. These are the works which have been translated and form the meager collection we enjoy today.

Not all historical documentation has disappeared

forever. Indeed, a few important documents have managed to escape destruction and obliteration and these, together with great thinkers and researchers, have allowed us to piece together a history of women: herstory. As far back as Sappho, women have been conscious of the fact that they have not been treated as equals with respect to men. Women have always, in the back of their minds, realized that their unfair treatment needed to be corrected and, as times changed, as thinking developed in different directions, as society flowed in different ways allowing for change, so women took advantage to push for equal rights, beginning with the right to vote, and followed with other petitions, always in the hope of improving their conditions. With the help of men sympathetic to their cause, women began to form themselves into a cohesive group transcending national boundaries: women in Europe, mainly France and England, knew what women in the United States were doing, and vice-versa, thanks to the transatlantic cable and rise in the travel industry.

The transatlantic cable may not have had anything to do directly with women per se, but it brought women together. The Anglo-American Telegraph Company completed its link from Newfoundland to Valentia Island to Queenstown in Ireland in 1866. Previous to this, women across the Atlantic had communicated but the cable now afforded a major impulse in massive women-to-women communication. Although communication through the cable was expensive, newspapers were given priority to carry their news from one end of the globe to the other and, in this way, news traveled at a much greater speed than ordinary mail, getting to different continents and diffusing news in a matter of minutes. Suddenly, small towns in rural United States knew what was happening, not only within the United States itself, but of what was going on in the United Kingdom. Women were able to disseminate ideas at a faster rate than before, plus there was the added bonus that with speed came quantity: thousands of women around the globe were brought together through this major advancement in technology.

Soon, another phenomenon arose. With so much to see and so much to learn about the four corners of the globe, migration and travel became more popular than ever. Between 1815 and 1932 over sixty million people migrated from European countries to North and South America, to New Zealand, and to Australia. Although revolutions, famines, and other events were the main causes of this mass migration, other causes, like explorations and subsequent visits to relatives, contributed to making it possible for women to travel to different countries. In these travels many women kept records, journals, memoirs, and travelogues; and they wrote autobiographies that were later published and disseminated to be read by other women in faraway places. Suddenly, women traveled more, escorted and unescorted by men, and took their own daring trips, some with other female companions who also kept records of places they visited.

The common root was that women from different backgrounds were brought together in international connections that finally gave way to an intricate international web of women who were able to convene and call for an international congress.

The fight for enfranchisement had begun—a fight that would span several decades until they achieved the desired goal: the right to vote—a right that was denied them and one which was believed would elevate women from their present status of inferior citizens to a more equal footing with men.

Changing Social Conditions

Temperance

As noted above, the women's rights movement was a gradual process of consciousness raising. Aside from the theories stated earlier, the women's rights movement can also be said to be heavily influenced by various reform movements of the time: temperance, anti-prostitution, peace, utopianism, and especially, abolition.

Religious advocates, especially Protestant and Quakers, desired new laws, progress, and the fulfillment of the individual. For example, the Protestant religion is founded on the belief that the individual, not the priest nor the church, is the one responsible for her/his own salvation. Although this is the theory, in practice, both Calvin and Luther believed firmly that women were inferior to men. However, with the Protestant Reformation, new extremist sects developed. These new extremists attacked conventional marriage, believed in free love, and advocated the independence of women. Protestants from England came to the United States, bringing cultural changes in terms of religion and social issues. Because the stereotype of women fell into the caring and nurturing role, these societies employed women to disseminate the Holy Word and to help other women in terms of education and nursing during epidemics and wars.

Female evangelists realized that women were equal to men both spiritually and intellectually. That being the case, then, women should enjoy the same opportunities as men. Devout Christians took note of the situation society was in. Social reforms became important.

One social evil that was making its presence felt was alcohol. American society was relying heavily on liquor because it was cheap, was not contaminated— water and milk were unsafe to drink due to tuberculosis—and it gave working people energy for hard physical labor. It was medicinal, too, because it could be used as an anesthetic and an analgesic and, furthermore, this wonderful magic potion also had the capacity to comfort in times of stress, which at that time, many people certainly needed. Alcohol became a panacea. Americans were spending millions of dollars on liquor. Saloons were flourishing to the point that the saloon became a curse rather than a place of solace. Wives became concerned over the amount of money and time husbands spent in their favorite drinking holes; the Church became concerned about the evil ways of alcohol and how it turned men into animals.

Women finally banded together and took over, because they were the only protectors of themselves, their families, and of their children against the daily abuse of alcohol. In a society where women were a part of man's property upon marriage, the abuse of alcohol, in its many forms, became an important issue. Women possessed no rights, not even over their children. How then was the American family to survive if the sole proprietor of earnings and property (both his and hers) was losing his money and mind to the intoxicating influence of alcohol?

Because women were seen as the guardians of spiritual and moral values within their homes, their duties became to try to persuade men against alcohol and to convert them back from drunkenness. The work began with Christian (male) preachers who, taking advantage of the idea that hearth and home were a woman's sphere, formed campaigns to get women actively involved in the temperance movement. Christian women were instructed to go out and visit establishments that sold alcohol. The women's task was to procure signatures from these distributors of alcohol with the idea that their signature would bind them legally to discontinue their sale of the evil drink. If the women were refused either entrance to the establishment or a signature for their petition, the women sang and prayed in front of those establishments and allowed no one to enter. This was the beginning of the Women's Christian Temperance Union (WCTU). The WCTU was formed by the first group of women who went out, however, no single person took credit for the organization's formation. Instead several names stand out as important within the group such as Jennie Willing, Emily Miller, and Frances Willard among others.

The WCTU became enormously important and intertwined itself with the destiny of the suffrage movement. It appealed to women who found a voice through it, and it quickly became the largest women's organization in the United States. At first, the WCTU served under the umbrella of the Protestant faith, but it soon acted independently—especially of male authority. In fact, for many women it became the "woman's church." In subsequent years, the WCTU promoted the Home Protection Vote by endorsing women's suffrage, and in this, and in other ways, they encouraged female participation in the public sphere. These women speakers were the ones who promoted and conveyed information about the suffrage movement.

Black women were allowed to participate until they grew to such numbers that they formed their own branch to help improve the conditions of African-American women. This example was closely followed by other groups that encompassed immigrants entering the United States in later years. By the end of the nineteenth century there were over two hundred thousand female members from all walks of life.

The WCTU served to eradicate a social evil and, at the same time, to educate women. As more and more women joined, the WCTU expanded to reach further and further into social issues. Poverty, a by-product of heavy drinking, was an inevitable outcome, and it immediately became part of the WCTU's agenda. Since many women had become such great orators, they took it upon themselves to speak for prison reforms too. They spoke of their concern for homeless children and of reforms concerning adoption laws as well as juvenile alcoholism and child abuse. And, because its members were female, the WCTU also fought for the civil rights of women, both in the workplace and at home.

At the same time, other religious groups were also cropping up. In England, Catherine Booth and her husband, William, co-founded the Salvation Army. Catherine Booth's most important work was the pamphlet she wrote entitled, *Female Ministry*, in which she upheld the belief that one's sex was irrelevant in the face of Christianity. This pamphlet is the cornerstone of the Salvation Army doctrine, clearly demarcating the role woman should take up within religion.

Catherine Booth was a devout feminist when she met her husband, a Methodist preacher. She did not share his views concerning the "weaker sex." Fortunately, they both believed fervently in social reforms. Catherine's first speech got a negative reception by the people who thought that women should be quiet in church. When Catherine took the stand unasked, her speech changed William's view of the subservient role women should play in the church.

The Salvation Army was finally founded, and it was Catherine who stood at the helm. Soon enough, the Booths were fighting the hostility of not only the general population, but also of the Church of England. The main complaint all round was that women were being elevated to the status of man, and the outcries were even fiercer when many, both men and women, realized that the Salvation Army female officer was allowed equal rights with a man.

Catherine organized the Food for the Million Shops, allowing poor people to buy, at a very low cost, a three-course meal and, on Christmas day, Catherine and her Army distributed hundreds of meals all around London. In the end, after much struggle, the Church of England accepted the work of the Salvation Army because they were working with the poor—an area that nobody had much cared about until then.

Catherine also became interested in what was called sweated labor—extremely low wages for extremely long hours of work in extremely poor working conditions. She was especially interested because the main population of sweat laborers were women and children. One such company that favored such labor practices was Bryant & May, match makers. They used a highly toxic yellow phosphorous in making the heads of matches. Catherine learned that many women working for Bryant & May suffered from phossy jaw or necrosis of the bone caused by the toxic fumes of dipping the match heads in the phosphorous. At first, workers suffered from painful toothaches and sometimes swelling of the gums, but over time, due to poor ventilation inside the factory buildings, the jaw abscessed, rotting the bone to the marrow until it had to be surgically repaired, which resulted in facial disfigurement. Some workers suffered convulsions and hemorrhage from the lungs; in some cases even death.

The whole process of dipping the matches, drying the heads, and packing the matches was fraught with the danger of phossy jaw. Similar match companies in the United States employed the same techniques with the same hazardous results on its workers. Even though the United States Congress passed the Match Act of 1912 to eliminate phossy jaw from the American population, it took much strength and campaigning for the Salvation Army to do the same in England.

Catherine Booth and co-worker Annie Besant took a personal interest in this occupational hazard, and together led strong campaigns against the use of yellow phosphorous. The sad part was that many women's lives could have been spared if the British had followed the example of other European countries, who at that stage, used totally harmless red phosphorous to make their matches. In the end, the Salvation Army, to counteract and pressure Bryant &

May into changing their policies, created and opened their own match factory, using red phosphorous, in 1891. Not only did the workers have safer working conditions, they had higher salaries than their rival Bryant & May. In the end, Bryant & May finally acceded into changing their working policies.

The Salvation Army, organized on a militaristic structure, appealed to people in ever increasing numbers. Finally, they marched into Milwaukee, Wisconsin and established the first mission in 1889. Not very popular at first, by 1922 they had established themselves through different drives for food for the destitute, shelter for the homeless, and even the Booth Home and Hospital for Unwed Mothers. With the help of the Salvation Army women found a voice and foothold for the already brewing woman's movement.

Abolition

Abolition is the oldest and best-known reform movement that tremendously influenced the women's movement—perhaps laying a solid base for the movement to emerge. At the same time, the Quakers were the ones instrumental in the quest for freedom of slaves. Although slavery was abolished in England in 1772, and the international slave trade was outlawed in 1807, as long as there was a trade market for certain commodities in Europe, (for example, cotton and sugar, among other slave-produced products), the United States slave traffic continued to flourish.

The Religious Society of Friends, known as

Quakers[11], was founded in England in the seventeenth century by George Fox. He taught people who cared to listen to his ideas that there was no need for a theologically trained priest or any such trained person to establish communion between God and one's own soul. He believed that everybody could get in touch with God without rites or any other ritual because everybody has inside her/himself an inner light supplied by the Holy Spirit. If everybody had this capacity, Fox maintained, then there was no need for sacraments nor for an established church. Furthermore, his teachings were opposed to war, and he believed that women and men had equal rights.

These non-conformist ideas set the Quakers apart in a country that had already given a home to Pilgrims running away from the persecution of their own countries. Pilgrims had already become established in the new land, and the arrival of the Quakers created a certain amount of animosity and discord. The Quakers, for their part, believed in radical ideas that clashed with the religion of the Pilgrims at first, especially in matters concerning women since the Pilgrims believed that women were to be obedient to their husbands, who were head of the family.

Although the establishment condemned and persecuted the Quakers for their radical ideas, the Quakers were not sanctioned or victimized by the simple fact that they upheld the national government. Nor were the Quakers mistreated or punished in any way for not taking an active part in any war. Social

11 According to the journal of George Fox, Justice Bennet of Derby 'was the first that called us Quakers, because I bade them tremble at the word of the Lord'. In Penney, Norman (ed) 2007 *The Journal of George Fox* by George Fox. Cosimo Classics, New York.

conditions differed in the new land, and with the passage of time, there grew more tolerance for other religions.

The Religious Society of Friends continued to attract a great number of people because they upheld social justice and an equality that no other denomination professed to have at that time. At a time in history when the United States was in social and religious turmoil, the Quakers offered an alternative solution to the troubles afflicting the lives of citizens. Their philanthropic work drew many members, especially since the Quakers embraced the issue of abolition, making it their goal to eradicate slavery. Among noted American abolitionists many names stand out: Lucretia Mott, the Grimké Sisters, Susan B. Anthony, Frederick Douglass, Thomas Garret, Theodore Weld, and many others.

Sarah and Angelina Grimké were two southern-born sisters who expanded their intellectual energies to encompass writing and speaking for women's rights as well as for abolition. Both were Quakers and, although outwardly the Quakers upheld such ideals as equality between the sexes, in reality, many Quakers, both men and women, preferred to see women away from the public sphere. The Quakers, exercising this equality of the sexes, encouraged women to take active roles by petitioning for signatures, canvassing, and organizing their own groups in support of anti-slavery petitions.

The Quakers grudgingly accepted the Grimké Sisters to speak publicly against abolition when they realized that their power lay in numbers—and women made a big bulk. The Quakers also realized that these two women could speak to slave women because of the common factor of being women. The Grimké Sisters being southern was an added bonus that suited the cause very well because Sarah and Angelina could reach a population with their public speeches that white males could not. The Grimké Sisters not only spoke for freedom of slaves, they also spoke for women's rights, creating staunch feminists in the process.

But before the Grimké Sisters were taken seriously for the beliefs they upheld, they had to go through a lot of internal fighting with the Quakers, so much so that, at one stage, they were asked to leave the women's issue out or else for them to renounce their membership with the Quakers.

Both sisters helped the abolitionist and feminist causes enormously by writing a number of tracts against slavery and for the rights of women. Angelina Grimké was the first American woman to address a state legislature. Although both were unwavering abolitionists and feminists, Angelina favored the abolitionist cause, while her sister, Sarah, concentrated more on the rights of women.

Angelina married Quaker and abolitionist, Theodore Weld, however, they did not totally agree on everything—especially women's rights. Nevertheless, they worked together in the abolitionist cause. From the start, Weld was against the rights of women because he believed the issue generated controversy, which, unfortunately, detracted from the anti-slavery cause. Needless to say, Angelina disagreed. In one of his letters to the Grimké Sisters, Theodore urged the Sisters to stay away from women's issues and to concentrate on the abolitionist cause only. He began his letter with:

> *My dear sisters,*
> *I had it in my heart to make a suggestion*
> *to you in my last letter about your course*
> *touching the 'rights of women', but it was*
> *crowded out by other matters perhaps of less*
> *importance . . .[12]*

This gave the Sisters a hierarchy of causes. To this letter Angelina wrote back:

> *The time to assert a right is the time when*
> *the right is denied.*

She went on to add:

> *. . . whatever is right for a man to do is*
> *morally right for a woman to do. I recognize*
> *no rights but human rights.[13]*

It was a constant struggle for the Sisters to try to convince not only Weld—husband and brother-in-law—but other officials that the support of women was of utmost importance in the cause they were fighting. They drew on the abolition issue for a parallel between the African slaves and female "enslavement." They declared that in the same way several years ago the idea of a future when slaves could think of becoming free was ludicrous, so, too, was the idea that someday

---

12 Theodore Weld to Sarah and Angelina Grimké, August 15, 1837 published in *The Letters of Theodore Weld, Angelina Grimké Weld and Sarah M. Grimké, 1822-1844*, Vol. I, Gilbert H. Barnes and Dwight L. Dumond, eds. (1934; reprint, New York: Da Capo Press, 1970), 425-432.
13 Ibid.

women would want their rights. Although freedom of slaves would take several more years, the seed of abolition was there, and it was only a matter of time before it became a reality. The Sisters had the same thought in mind for the emancipation of women.

Both sisters refused to be silent and submissive because their voices needed to be heard if all men and women were to be free one day. It was these continuous arguments that won them their place in the cause, and they were finally allowed to exert their strength in the anti-slavery campaign.

Being untiring in their fight, they were not satisfied merely with the canvassing and petitioning that men assigned them to do. They were very clear that before they set out to speak against slavery they first had to have a safe place as women if they sought effectiveness in other areas. They traveled throughout the north, giving lectures concerning their experiences with slavery and the need for abolition. At the same time, they spoke of women and their natural rights. They were very often ridiculed and abused, but they continued their work, denouncing slavery and race prejudice and upholding the view that women, whether white or black, held a natural bond: that of being women.

This led to further attacks from the public in general to which the Sisters countered by writing their letters and tracts such as *Letters on the Equality of the Sexes*, which was a series of letters addressed to the President of the Abolitionist Society, and in which Sarah defended the rights of women to the public platform. *American Slavery as It Is: Testimony of a Thousand Witnesses*, on the other hand, is a collection of newspaper stories written by southern newspaper

editors and edited by the Sisters. They also wrote
*Epistle to the Clergy of the Southern States, Appeal to
the Woman of the Nominally Free States,* and many
others, including the correspondence between the
Sisters and Theodore Weld.

Both sisters led full and rich lives, Angelina
bearing three children and finally retiring from public
life, but, nevertheless, remaining an active abolitionist
and feminist. In their old age, they both attempted to
vote when the Fifteenth Amendment was introduced.
Although this amendment did not grant women
anything, they nevertheless lived an event in history
that was to mark the beginning of a movement that
would fight for the rights of women.

Other Influences

The nineteenth century was a century of great
insight and major upheaval with different groups
of people and foundations working toward social
improvements and against social injustices. Congress
was seeing petitions urging the prohibition of alcohol
as well as being bombarded by petitions for better
living conditions and prison reforms. At the same
time, a huge anti-slavery campaign was underway.
For the American society, the 1840s mark a milestone
when women realized, for all their campaigning and
lobbying in the anti-slavery movement, they had been
excluded from the World Anti-Slave Convention
held in London. The irony of it was that women had
worked hard alongside of men, and now their work
would not be recognized but simply usurped because
the convention was for men only. The idea that

women could not even attend, let alone speak, made Elizabeth Cady Stanton realize how unrepresented women were.

The 1840s also saw women fighting for the Married Women's Property Bill in the state of New York[14]—a bill that gave wives a host of rights, including the right to have their own wages and the right to own property in their own names. It gave widows legal access to their husbands' personal estates, the right to an equal say with their husbands about their children, and the right to sue in court. Although one of the earliest married women's property acts dates to 1809, enacted in Connecticut, it basically only allowed women to write wills. With the passage of years the majority of the states passed similar acts, and then, after New York, many other states modified their acts to grant women controls they had not had before. In essence, the New York Act altered the husbands' privileges granted by previous principles.

The 1840s also saw the Women's Rights Convention held in Seneca Falls, New York in 1848, the biggest triumph for women thus far and, for some, the official date when the women's movement really began.

Seneca Falls initiated a long series of women's rights conventions all across the United States. Led by Elizabeth Cady Stanton, Susan B. Anthony, and others associated with the anti-slavery movement, such as Lucy Stone and Lucretia Mott, they continued to work, not, interestingly enough with the idea of voting, but rather petitioning for women's economic subjection in civil law. Of importance were: that

14 See appendix 4 for an excerpt of the Act.

women control their own earnings and that women remain in custody of their children upon divorce. However, soon after, these women began to seriously talk about the right to vote.

What happened, again, was yet another example of the consequences elicited by the social turmoil affecting the country. Not only were the Quakers working for freedom of slaves, other groups and societies, like the Female Anti-Slavery Society, took up the cause too. In 1833, Lucretia Mott organized and led abolitionist rallies and, although much of the debate around the issue centered over the fear of intermarriage and mixing of black and white, history shows what this fear and hatred did to deter the cause.

At the same time, because of the social denial that women should speak in public, many women realized just how persecuted and discriminated upon they were. Even Thomas Jefferson, in the early 1800s, had stated that women should not read books and that women's education should concentrate on such things as dancing, drawing, and music. In other words, women should concentrate on ornaments and the amusements of life.

These were the sentiments of society toward women. With such injustices, Sarah Grimké had no option but to write her *Letters on the Equality of the Sexes,* asking ". . . no favors for my sex. I surrender not our claim to equality. All I ask of our brethren is, that they will take their feet from off our necks, and permit us to stand upright on that ground which God designed us to occupy."[15] The discrimination that

15 Grimke, Sarah Moore. 2007. *Letters On The Equality Of The Sexes And The Condition Of Woman: Addressed To Mary S. Parker, President Of The Boston Female Anti-Slavery Society.* Kessinger Publishing, LLC. (Letter 2, July 17, 1837)

women were suffering, both in society and within the abolitionist movement, had become intolerable. This was the turning point for Elizabeth Cady Stanton and Lucretia Mott, who, with several other women, decided that they should organize themselves to advocate for women's rights.

In getting together, these first women realized that although the American Revolution had been fought to win a rightful freedom, women had not won anything at all, notwithstanding the fact that they had actively participated in the attainment of that freedom. Stanton, Mott, and others decided to hold a convention to discuss the social, civil, and religious conditions, as well as the rights of women. As the meeting place, they chose the Wesleyan Chapel in Seneca Falls, New York, on July 19th and 20th of the year 1848.

A Declaration of Sentiments was drafted using the format of the Declaration of Independence, and the same wording was used to push home the notion that all men and women were created equal. It was Stanton's idea, and it proved to be a very good one since she made use of the symbol of liberty—a symbol that all Americans fervently upheld and continue to uphold.

In this Declaration, the areas of life where women were treated unjustly were carefully enumerated in eighteen paragraphs, followed by a section delineating the resolutions.

Many people joined the cause, and just as many opposed it. The convention went on as planned and, although most of the resolutions were unanimously endorsed, the one that met with the most controversy was the ninth, the one which would secure women the elective franchise. Even women friends of Stanton's were shocked at the idea. It barely passed by a tiny majority, and this was due to those who argued that if blacks were free, then women had the right to be free too, and to choose the rulers that made the laws.

A period of uncertainty, backlash, and abuse ensued in which newspapers openly ridiculed the Declaration and, such was the backlash, that many who had signed in favor of the Declaration now withdrew their signatures—though most stayed on and endured the abuse. As fate would have it, such was the negative publicity that it had a reverse effect and, many far away towns totally unconnected with what was going on in New York, heard of the Declaration. Suddenly, what started as negative publicity became, in reality, a spreading of news in which a group of women had dared to stand up for themselves. The result was the population at large was alerted to the issue and thousands, far and wide, joined the growing group.

Soon, conventions followed in every part of the country. In Akron, Ohio, Sojourner Truth gave her speech in which she stated that ". . . if the first woman God ever made was strong enough to turn the world upside down all alone, women together ought to be able to turn it back, and get it right side up again."[16] In Cincinnati, Lucretia Mott spoke of rights of women in education, in marriage, in religion, and in life in general. On her part, Elizabeth Cady Stanton spoke many times of woman as a slave who is deemed property by taking the name of the owner, her husband, just like a Southern slave. Suffrage, then, became the chief goal of the women's rights movement because if women could vote, then they could have more rights.

16 See appendix 5 for a transcript of her speech "Ain't I a Woman."

Another important figure at the time who was central to the women's right to vote was Susan B. Anthony. Known as The Mother of Us All, Anthony was born in 1820 in Adams, Massachusetts, therefore very much a part of the social chaos that afflicted the country at that stage. She was the daughter of Quakers and was soon involved in the antislavery and temperance movements in New York where her family had moved.

The first time Anthony came into contact with inequalities regarding men and women was in her own home. Her father was the owner of some cotton mills, which had mainly girls as workers. Anthony learned how to weave from Sally A. Hyatt, a skilled weaver who also taught the newcomers their new trade. When Anthony's father appointed a man as supervisor of a mill, she was baffled, and she asked her father why he had not appointed Sally. After all, Sally knew her job well, and she was the person who best fit the job. Anthony's father replied that the job of a supervisor was only a male job. From then on, Anthony was very much aware of the inequalities between men and women. Later on, she was to give up being a Quaker because of the same outlook of pretending to uphold equality between the sexes. She found out that equality for the Quakers meant that women could work, indeed they had the same right as a man, but she found out that this so-called equality had limitations: women were only allowed to work in certain areas such as teaching, nursing, farm, and factory help, or as maids. Every other job that held some form of responsibility was automatically designated as male. A worse blow came when she realized that women's wages were lower than their male counterparts. In fact, she left her job as teacher because she realized that male teachers earned almost four times her salary. She refused to idolize men, and she turned down many suitors because she also refused to become a simple housewife.

It was about this time that she became involved in the anti-slavery movement, the temperance movement, and the women's rights movement. She admired the Grimké Sisters and Lucretia Mott in their efforts to help slaves escape from the South to the North and joined them wholeheartedly.

Anthony attended the Woman's Rights Convention in Seneca Falls, where she met Stanton. Their friendship grew, and they fought side by side in their women's rights crusade. Anthony devoted herself almost exclusively to the women's rights cause, at the same time, speaking and writing zealously against abortion because she saw it as an imposition of men onto women.

From 1868 to 1870 she was the proprietor of a weekly newspaper, *The Revolution,* edited by Elizabeth C. Stanton. The motto of the paper was: *The True Republic—men, their rights and nothing more; women, their rights and nothing less.*

Although the newspaper was to die after barely two years, it gave these two women a platform from which to promote women's suffrage as well as question the unfairness in the institutions of marriage, law, and organized religion. In the paper, they also urged women to demand equal pay at work. Needless to say, they endured a lot of abuse from society at large, but, resolved, these women strived forward.

1865 saw the end of the Civil War and the Thirteenth Amendment to abolish slavery was passed.

Since the amendment was ratified, many felt that the anti-slavery groups should disband. Others disagreed since, for some, this was the best platform from which to fight for women's rights. Sojourner Truth[17] was one of these women who disagreed to disband. For her, colored men had gotten rights but colored women had not because, although they were free from slavery, they were now slaves to the black man. The urgency for women's rights became stronger when, in 1868, the Fourteenth Amendment was ratified, giving men of color full citizenship. Again, women were left out. The amendment deliberately did not include women.

This was a blow for many women, especially for Elizabeth C. Stanton and Susan B. Anthony who had been friends of Frederick Douglass and other male abolitionists for several years. They felt that their efforts had been sabotaged by men, and so, in 1865, these two women, with other followers, started the National Women's Suffrage Association (NWSA) for women only. A parallel group, a mixed gender group, the American Woman Suffrage Association (AWSA) was started that same year with Lucy Stone at the head. Both groups, basically, sought the same ends, but they were constantly at loggerheads with each other. The AWSA was organized primarily in the north with middle- and upper-class members. They were less militant, and were only concerned with the vote, leaving out any other issues. The NWSA, on the other hand, went south to organize working-class and colored women. They condemned the Fourteenth Amendment (and later on the Fifteenth) as a blatant injustice to women. They were also involved with

---

17 See appendix 2 for a short biography.

other issues such as divorce and discrimination in employment and pay.

Another blow came in 1870 when the Fifteenth Amendment was ratified. This amendment gave black men the right to vote, and again, women were deliberately not included. This gave Stanton and Anthony renewed strength to concentrate on women's issues and to keep on fighting for the right to vote. Frederick Douglass, once an ardent advocate of women's rights, suddenly was no longer concerned with women and refused to work for women's suffrage. He concentrated on protecting the rights that were already won for the black man. Stanton and Anthony saw the need to campaign state by state and, in 1878, after a lot of hard work, Anthony managed to get Congress to introduce an amendment in favor of women franchise.

But they lost. Again.

It soon became clear that the AWSA and NWSA should be working together, and after several negotiations orchestrated by Anthony, the two organizations merged in 1890, creating the National American Woman Suffrage Association (NAWSA). At the head of this new group were women like Elizabeth Cady Stanton, Susan B. Anthony, Carrie Chapman Catt, Amelia Bloomer, Frances Willard, and Matilda Joslyn Gage, among many others. The group was mostly conservative, wealthy, and non-black, which, again, opened a rift between factions. The internal disputes and criticisms were many because suffrage was about women regardless of color or socio-economic position. Meanwhile, other women in the group felt that women of color needed to fight for their civil rights separate from women getting the vote. Aside from that, one faction wanted to concentrate on the vote only while the other faction wanted to bring in other issues, such as religion and marriage, which also held women in bondage. These internal disputes hampered the women's movement and frustrated Anthony to no end. She felt that women had not yet achieved equality with men because women were always focusing on issues other than for their own freedom.

Regardless of these internal disputes, they managed to strive on, and, state by state, they slowly but surely, gained the right to vote. Congress still would not pass the Amendment. Between 1870 and 1910 there were seventeen state referenda concerning this amendment and, during these years, many more women became involved in this nationwide quest. Working with journals such as *Women Voter, The Women's Journal, Woman Citizen,* and many others, suffragists waged a huge national campaign. In 1893, women got the vote in Colorado, then Utah in 1896, Idaho came next in 1896, followed by Washington (1910), California (1911), Arizona (1912), Kansas (1912), Oregon (1912), Illinois (1913), Nevada (1914), and Montana (1914).

In 1872, Anthony and a group of women tried to vote in the presidential elections in New York. They were arrested and fined, proving that women were still second-class citizens. But the turn of the century saw some changes. A new generation of leaders brought a different insight into the women's suffrage movement. For example, Alice Paul came back from England, bringing new ideas for tactics employed by British women in their fight for suffrage. Anthony and her followers put these new ideas to practice by organizing themselves better and by lobbying in the nation's capital. Daughters of the original leaders, such as Harriot E. Blatch (Stanton's daughter), appealed to the younger generation, radicals, and working-class women. All of them picketed, marched, and protested. Some, like Alice Paul and her followers, chained themselves to the White House fences. When they were arrested and sent to jail they went on hunger strikes.

The women endured rotten eggs, catcalls, and other abuse. Many of them were burned in effigy. Once again, in 1914 the amendment was introduced before Congress, and again it was refused. Finally, on the twenty-sixth of August, 1920, the Nineteenth Amendment was passed. It was a great victory, almost a storybook victory. Only one state, Tennessee, was left to cast its vote. The state did not want to pass it, but they took a straw poll. The vote came down to only one senator, a young man who had promised his mother many years earlier when Susan B. Anthony had knocked on their door, that if his vote was the deciding one, then he would vote in favor. He honored his promise. After seventy years of struggle, women finally won the right to vote.

SECOND WAVE FEMINISM

After the Vote

Contrary to popular belief, what is termed the Second Wave of the feminist movement did not start in the 1960s. It is even said that the term Second Wave was coined by Marsh Lear referring to the renewed feminist activity that emerged in the sixties all over Europe, Britain, and the United States. But what needs to be realized is that the second wave of feminism started where the first wave left off. In other words, the first wave was the crucial paving stone necessary to allow the next generation of women to continue pushing forward in order to give women the same benefits that men enjoyed.

Winning the vote did not satisfy all the women who had lobbied and rallied in the 1920s, though for many it was the end of the struggle. Alice Paul, leader of the National Woman's Party (NWP), understood clearly that the struggle was an ongoing affair and this was not the time to sit back and rest on one's laurels. Because she was aware of the dangers of having come this far to suddenly lose everything, she strove on by drafting the Equal Rights Amendment for the United States Constitution in which she argued that, in the United States, men and women had equal rights no matter where they lived.

Section 1 of the ERA states: "Equality for rights under the law shall not be denied or abridged by the United States or by any state on account of sex." This was, in fact, a rewording of the Lucretia Mott

Amendment[18] introduced in 1923 in Seneca Falls in the celebration of the seventy-fifth anniversary of the 1848 Woman's Rights Convention.

In 1943, Alice Paul rewrote the ERA to what is now called the Alice Paul Amendment, which reflects the Fifteenth and the Nineteenth Amendments: "Equality of rights under the law shall not be denied or abridged by the United States or by any state on account of sex."

The Equal Rights Amendment, using these same words one way or another, was introduced in Congress session after session until it passed in 1972. Little did any of these women know at the time that it would be so difficult for the states to ratify it. Though women lobbied, rallied, went on hunger strikes, committed acts of disobedience, and campaigned, the ERA was not ratified by enough states to pass. That year, although approved by the U.S. Senate and the House of Representatives, the ERA fell short by sixteen votes. They barely had twenty-two out of the necessary thirty-eight ratifications. Although the rallying women knew they had seven years by law before the deadline on the ratification process, for some, hope slowly eroded away as several states slowed down in their decisions and opposing factions made their resistance and disagreement felt.

Anti-ERA groups mushroomed in an attempt to halt the ratification of what they considered to be a denial of women's rights. Opposition activists, organized mainly by right-wing religious groups,

18 At this convention, Alice Paul introduced the Lucretia Mott Amendment, which read: "Men and women shall have equal rights throughout the United States and every place subject to its jurisdiction."

believed that the privacy rights of women would be overturned if the amendment was passed. They also claimed that the ERA would allow for such issues as the right for homosexuals to marry, and for the endorsement of abortion rights, among other matters of concern.

Advocates of the ERA saw their hopes dim as they witnessed states postponing their decisions, other states losing, or, in the case of Illinois, a change in the laws whereby a majority of three-fifths was needed to ratify the amendment.

Still, year after year, pro-ERA activists kept up the fight through petitioning, rallies, picketing, walkathons, and mimicking other tactics employed by the radical suffragettes of yesteryear. Inevitably, the deadline—set for 1979—approached and there was no resolution in sight for pro-ERA activists. In an attempt to pressure Congress, NOW organized a march in Washington D.C where over one hundred thousand people participated. Together with other supporting groups they appealed to Congress to grant them an extension. Congress conceded by granting a three-year extension that would take pro-ERA lobbyists to 1982.

Ironically, history was repeated. Like the Fourteenth Amendment, ERA fell short of three pivotal states. Though women were part of legislature in 1982, their numbers were too few in crucial posts to maintain the pressure and help the ERA along. A large part of the population were sympathetic to the cause, but were not yet willing to support the idea of giving women the same constitutional rights as men. And it was too controversial for politicians. Once again, as with all issues concerning women, their struggles were met with the controversial element, hampering any forward movement.

In the years between the passing of the Nineteenth Amendment and the Second World War, women concentrated mainly on issues concerning health, education for all, and housing, to name a few. Small groups of women within their own cities, towns, and communities continued in their quests to achieve whatever goals were in their agendas.

In 1939, war broke out in Europe and, although the United States initially took no part in it, soon it became adamant for them to enter the war to help the Europeans fight against the Nazi ideology that threatened to engulf the whole continent. Peace was finally achieved after a costly six-year war in which millions of lives were unnecessarily lost, millions of U.S. dollars were unnecessarily spent, and millions of people now faced the arduous task of rebuilding towns, cities, and whole countries from the rubble that remained.

Interestingly enough, the Second World War and its aftermath sparked off a renewed awareness of women's position in society. To say that waves of feminism comprised the decades of the so-and-so to the so-and-so would be unfair to all the women who kept up the struggle to make changes happen. The history of the women's movement should best be seen as a continuum, perhaps with sporadic downs, but never fully at a standstill. From first wave to second wave there has been no hiatus. On the contrary. Women have continued to have meetings, to rally, to lobby, to hold petition drives, and, above all, to hold nonviolent resistance to social pressure to help the status of women from slipping back to colonial days.

It can be safely said that the issues addressed in these different eras or waves (which for the sake of convenience are called first and second) have been different. Following conventional norm, then, the first wave addressed a very important issue which was the cornerstone for subsequent waves: the demand for equal treatment within the establishment and within male institutions.

Rosie the Riveter

Wining the vote for women in the 1920s meant that they had won a battle. Nobody thought to go any further in trying to win the proverbial war until circumstances around the world exploded. A real war, World War II, threatened the lives of millions around the world. World War II had different repercussions in different countries, but there was one repercussion that was identical in all those countries that went to war: men were drafted. As a consequence, there was a lack of men in towns—they were away, fighting the war. With men gone, hundreds of job vacancies were left open. Suddenly, societies needed somebody to take over those jobs. The only solution, the only available human resource, were women.

Due to the precarious situation of most countries involved in the war, many factories turned from manufacturing their original products (washing machines, electro-domestic appliances, bicycles, etc.) to manufacturing bombs, airplanes, armored cars, ammunition, and a host of other products of utmost importance for fighting the war.

Up until then, women all over the world, and

especially in the United States, had been limited to housework (sewing, cooking), nursing, caring for the old, or, if working in factories, employed in light-manufacturing jobs that paid next to nothing.

Suddenly, with a diminished number of men in the workforce, countries needed to take measures to offset the deficit of male workers. Though most countries allowed women to join the workforce freely, President Roosevelt went a step further. He created two organizations that worked hand in hand to recruit women. The first organization was the War Manpower Commission (WMC) which assured the most effective mobilization of the nation's manpower and, at the same time, utilized to its maximum the resources of this manpower to better serve the nation in its prosecution of the war. The second organization, the Office of War Information (OWI) was especially appointed to disseminate propaganda to call women to war. At first, managers, husbands, male co-workers, and even women themselves were reluctant to take on these vacant posts. However, after the propaganda, many women working in low-paid jobs (for example, laundries) saw the advantages of switching to these glorified higher-paying posts. For other women, the propaganda appealed to their patriotic feelings. Still other women, as first-time workers, saw this as their chance to enter the workforce, and others who had lost their jobs during the Depression saw this as an opportunity to join work again.

For many women, the idea of working outside the home was totally foreign, and many needed a lot of encouragement.

Westinghouse Electric, an American power company of the time, spurred loyalty and duty toward the nation with the idea of creating a mythical woman who would represent the women of the United States. The idea was hailed as excellent. Posters were created and plastered all over the country. The woman depicted in the poster was Rosie the Riveter.

A song was released in 1943, written by Rudd Evans and John J. Loeb, to accompany the posters in the campaign for recruiting women into factory war jobs. The song had an upbeat rhythm, and was sung by the Four Vagabonds—a group that was making waves at the time. The name "Rosie the Riveter" was nothing more than a catchy alliteration, and soon, together with the posters, successfully hailed women into the workforce. The lyrics were appropriate:

> *All day long, whether rain or shine,*
> *She's part of the assembly line,*
> *She's making history working for victory,* .
> *Rosie, Rosie, Rosie, Rosie, Rosie, Rosie the Riveter*

The poster depicted a woman in blue-jean overalls, bandana, sweating, and sporting a big attitude. In short, Rosie was brawny, and she was larger than life. She was a beacon, and women aspired to be her. There were several posters depicting Rosie differently—with spanners, rivet machine, welder, etc.—but they all had the same message of asking women to serve their country because their country needed them. And Rosie was made to appeal to both men and women. She had a smile on her face, she took pleasure from her factory job—sweaty though it may have been— and she still maintained her femininity as depicted by the defined eyebrows, the nail polish, the lipstick, and so forth. Interestingly enough, she does not wear a wedding ring in any of these posters. Each poster had a caption designed to appeal to national patriotism, with slogans such as: "Women in the War. We cannot win without them," or "Count on US," and several others. Rosie even appeared in movie theaters as advertisements between films or news releases.

Because defense and factory jobs were not the only jobs needed to help out in the war, the Roosevelt administration turned again to Norman Rockwell (creator of Rosie) to come up with another image that emphasized different types of employment, such as farmer, conductor, mechanic, telephone operator, elevator operator, ticket agent, and many posts left vacant and in desperate need of workers. This new image, which was released barely three months after Rosie, was called Liberty Girl. This woman was a representational collage of different professions. For a start, she wore patriotic clothes (pants were red and white, while the shirt was white spangles against blue), she wore a nurse or a police hat, and over her shoulders she carried an item that represented the different types of civilian jobs (bag with milk bottles, hoe, wrench, dustpan, earphones, etc). In short, it was the portrait of a jack-of-all-trades. This image appeared on the September 4, 1943 issue of the *Saturday Evening Post*. The caption read: The More Women at Work the Sooner We Win.

Unfortunately, this image was not as captivating as Rosie, and soon this poster was abandoned and replaced by posters depicting each profession, such as a young girl saluting from behind a typewriter. The caption read: Victory Awaits on your Fingers. And many other such posters.

In the United States alone, more than seven

million women joined the workforce in industries that ranged from lumber and steel mills, to shipyards and airplane hangars. Women became physicists, chemists, lawyers, police officers, and a host of other professions that, up until then, had been deemed as unsuitable for a woman. Anywhere that needed a workforce, one would find women by the dozen. Factory jobs assimilated the bulk of female workers, both white and African-American. Many women worked in poor conditions, and they were paid less than their male counterparts. For example, in 1944, the male average weekly salary was approximately $54.65. Women, for the same labor and under the same conditions, averaged $31.21 a week. But they did not complain. They were proud of their hidden strength and power in the face of adversity, while at the same time serving their country.

Since women were better at fine motor skills due to sewing—or so it was claimed—they were employed in tasks that necessitated small hands and deft fingers, such as in the making of bombs, fuses for bombs, radio components, candles, and many other tasks. Although none of the women employed in these jobs had any formal training, they were hired and trained on the spot. And it was this very factor that companies and factories used as an excuse to pay women much less than their male counterparts. Women, it was stated, were not certified and proof of it was that they were trained upon arrival. This argument ensured that nobody would complain, and, in any case, there would not have been anybody to listen to their complaints.

Many women chose to go to night school—after a full day at work and taking care of their homes—

to understand the basics of what their new jobs entailed, but the majority did not. Because of the state of emergency in the country, it did not matter if they had a diploma or not as long as they knew what they were doing. Formally trained or not, all of the women endured the hardships of their jobs: danger from chemicals or explosives, heights without proper safety, plus the added pressure of emergency that urged them to work faster, oftentimes putting their lives at unnecessary risks. It has been recorded that over half-a-million women were permanently disabled, and that nearly one hundred thousand lost their lives during the course of their jobs.

At the same time the United States and other countries needed the help of women and purposely recruited them, women had to endure sexual harassment, social discrimination, denigration, and resentment from men who had not been drafted for whatever reason and who had no option but to work in the factories. Not all men were happy that women were working side by side with them in jobs that had, until then, been traditionally male. In some cases, men deliberately messed up by welding the wrong pieces together, and women had no alternative but to fix these mistakes by redoing the whole piece before they could do their own work. To endure these unbearable conditions, women joined the unions, but again, for some, the unions afforded some sort of relief, while for others they did not. The paradox was that at the same time that women were urged to join the workforce to win the war, they were seen as threats to men in those jobs.

All this said, World War II was pivotal in influencing and changing the lives of many women.

The most important lesson to be learned was the extent of a woman's capacities, abilities, and endurance which showed women that they were as capable—if not more so—of doing exactly the same jobs as men. Secondly, World War II gave women an opportunity to see themselves as useful contributors to society. Thirdly, World War II allowed women to be independent, and to be able to earn a salary for the work they performed, be it as nurses in the WAC (Women's Auxiliary Corps) or as welders in a factory. Lastly, by doing all of the above, they were out of the house, a liberation that undermined marriage and family life which, historically, were the traditional roles of women. As an added bonus, women were able to break the mold of social conventions. Women's identities suddenly were wrapped around themselves, not around their husbands or children.

The end of the war was not the end of hardship for women. Having found their new freedom, many women expected to remain in their jobs. But it soon became apparent that this was not to be so. As soon as the war ended, a new campaign, divergent to Rosie, began. This new campaign, once again, turned to propaganda, this time telling women to go home. Once more, the government resorted to posters, ads, and radio shows to urge women to go back to their homes and to look after their hero husbands returned from the war, and to focus on their family. Overnight, Rosie no longer existed. She vanished into thin air.

It was a perfectly orchestrated governmental maneuver. As far back as a year before the end of the war, both the OWI and the WMC had stopped recruiting women and had begun disseminating new propaganda. The new propaganda urged women to leave factory work and any other work which was not in accordance with the traditional feminine jobs of yore—nursing, teaching, and the caring field in general. Many women left voluntarily, having served their country, but many were laid off to make room for returning male workers. By 1946, over three million women had left the workforce and returned to their homes.

Sadly nobody bothered to ask women what they had experienced, what they had felt about doing war jobs, or what they had gone through. They were simply thanked and asked to go home—no recognition given, no questions asked. A new image of the American woman emerged. At great pains, the American government began the campaign for the All New American Family.

The 1960s

After the war, the whole world seemed to settle down peacefully—at least for a while. Countries rebuilt themselves from the wasted rubble left by the ravages of a long war and economies grew. Just when the whole world was picking up economic and social momentum, the unthinkable happened. A group of students in Ann Arbor, Michigan, disappointed with the youth branch of the socialist educational organization of the time (Student League for Industrial Democracy) decided to dissociate themselves totally from the parent organization by creating their own group to fully address the expectations and current mood of the campuses. They called themselves Students for a Democratic Society (SDS) and held their first meeting in 1960.

The SDS became an instant hit within the student population while, at the same time, urging all Americans to join in the cause. Their manifesto asked that every single American be given the right to become an active participant in all those economic, social, and political issues that only a few elite were a part of. The manifesto demanded that American citizens needed their voices to be heard in the decision-making policies and activities that shaped the nation, while at the same time, the SDS also criticized the American society for focusing on such issues as military strength, racism, and materialism.

In California, students held rallies and sit-ins, protesting their restrictions within universities and demanding their right to conduct political activities on campuses across the country.

Activism became a public issue with different groups protesting every aspect of society and spurring further liberal and radical thinking in different areas of life. Student movement demonstrations soon merged with those groups protesting the Vietnam War. Anti-war demonstrators filled the news as they clashed violently against the police. Images of police beating students unleashed a wave of violence that climaxed in May 1970 at Kent State University (Ohio) when a troop of National Guards gunned down four student protesters.

Social change was inevitable. Colleges and universities became more relaxed in their dress codes, in recruiting more students from minority groups, and in allowing students to freely exercise more rights.

Growing disillusionment with governments, violence, petitioning for more rights, and a host of other pertinent issues became the order of the day during the fifties, sixties, and into the seventies. Given the social unrest that characterized the times, it was inevitable that the feminist movement was affected in unprecedented ways. Indeed, it gathered new strength and new voices, and shifted from accessing rights (first wave) to developing autonomy and differences from men (second wave). The women that constituted this second wave of feminism were women of their times, affected by the current events of their culture and taking advantage of general social changes. They formed a second wave of feminism that was characterized by a liberal tendency that claimed that only biology differentiated men from women, and that these differences were to be blamed on the socialization process of society—schools, mass media, family values, etc. Meanwhile, another set of feminists emerged at the same time—a more radical one who blamed capitalism and patriarchy for the existing inequalities, exploitation, and subjugation of women, both black and white.

In order to develop autonomy from men, the new wave of feminists used different resources to debate the psychoanalytic and social theories that were becoming a trend to create a new standpoint from which to view "woman." As women became more organized, more assertive, and more at the forefront of their fight, they critiqued traditional theories postulated by different disciplines which had, until then, been male oriented. A brief analysis of some disciplines are as follows:

- Anthropology – is criticized for establishing differences between the sexes.

- Economics – have never valued women's activities, especially those carried out in the domestic and informal sectors.
- History – has always been recorded from the male point of view, leaving out women and their achievements.
- Law – has always supported male superiority and dominance, particularly white male.
- Literature – has always ignored women's contributions to the point that many women wrote under male pseudonyms to be published.
- Media – have always misrepresented women and upheld social standards which are by definition male oriented.
- Medicine – has always objectified women and has, for the most part, ignored women's anatomy and issues concerning women's health.
- Psychoanalysis – upholds male definitions of women and "the feminine."
- Science in general – women have always been marginalized due to the fact that this is a "male" discipline.
- Sociology – uses gender as a category to discriminate and define women, and what important role they play in society.

The second wave, using the first wave as a platform from which to build further, focused on issues such as reproduction, sexual preferences or orientation, social representations, family issues, the environment, and a host of other topics pertinent to the times. It is important to note that as changes began within these disciplines, language became an issue of importance as well. Language was hailed as gendered, and there was a determined strive toward gender-neutral language to take out the biases reflected in a flawed social system. New terms and slogans appeared in the language, employed first by feminists, then by society at large. The suffix "man" was replaced by either "woman" or "person," (e.g. chairperson, businessperson, etc.) and similar other changes were brought into the language. New terminology like "sexism," "consciousness raising," and the famous slogan of "personal is political" became household words and phrases, and contributed to impelling women forward. Magazines, newspapers, books, and other forms of publications mushroomed, opening the doors to female expression in different forms.

From all this was a major outcome: a new Women's Rights Movement. Grassroots projects by women from all walks of life, backgrounds, and professions took on a new meaning. Shelters for battered women, rape centers, crises centers, women's clinics, children clinics, and other organizations sprang to aid women to try to abolish sexual abuse and domestic violence, to help women become educated in birth control and family planning, and above all, to work outside their homes for a salary equal to that of men.

The Women's Rights Movement brought change to the way of thinking for the population at large. The main impact was in the financial liberation of women. Thanks to the Second World War, the Roosevelt administration had taken women out of the kitchen and out of the home and had placed her in the workforce.

Civil Rights Movement

Many women took advantage of the work experience they had gained during the Second World War to seek jobs, now that the economy was, once again, booming in the United States. Returning to work made women aware of the rift between their salaries and their male counterparts. Also, many men were not prepared to work alongside women, and women found themselves harassed and humiliated in every aspect of work. Finally, women began to voice their discontent with their unequal social and economic status. These years right after the war were crucial for the feminist movement.

Another area of tremendous social unrest brewing at the same time in the United States was the Civil Rights Movement.

The racial issue heightened soon after the American Civil War when most states in the South passed anti-African-American legislations. These became known as Jim Crow laws. Jim Crow was a rigid series of laws that relegated the African-American population to second-class citizens with no recourse. The system was such that black people could be degraded in public, and newspapers could allude to them in denigrating terms. Blacks were said to be inferior to whites and, therefore, sexual relations between blacks and whites were strictly discouraged with severe repercussions, since such a union would only produce an inferior race that would undermine American society. In short, the Jim Crow laws discriminated against African-Americans in all areas of life, from education to social life to leisure to economic opportunity.

Restaurants, theaters, hotels, cinemas, and public baths were clearly segregated, as were all modes of public transport. Jim Crow laws were a system that justified violence, real and threatened. For example, a black male could not offer to shake hands with a white male. This act implied that the black male was socially equal to the white male. Needless to say, a black male could not offer his hand or arm to help a white woman, because he risked being accused of rape.[19] If an African-American violated a Jim Crow law, whites could physically beat the "offender" without any legal recourse from the "offender." Violence was instrumental for Jim Crow, and because the Jim Crow criminal justice system (police, prosecutors, juries, judges, and prison wardens) was all white, an African-American stood no chance. The most extreme forms of violence unpunished by the law were lynchings. Lynchings were public, sadistic, and, oftentimes, the lynched African-American died.

The racial issue in the United States finally came to a boiling point in the mid-fifties. Race relations were extremely tense since, up until then, there were still four permissible major acts of discrimination, mainly in the southern states: racial segregation, voter suppression, denial of economic opportunity, and private acts of violence. In May 1954 Brown v. Board of Education tipped the balance. Many people, frustrated with the poorly attempted efforts on behalf of the government to implement desegregation, began a non-violent resistance—what was called civil disobedience—and activists employed different tactics to show their disagreement, from sit-ins to boycotts to marches. In the case of Brown v. Board of Education, the court ruled that separate education meant that it was unequal education and cultivated a sense of inferiority in black students,

19 See appendix 6 for Jim Crow laws, as compiled by the Martin Luther King, Jr., National Historic Site Interpretive Staff.

especially children. The court ruled that the system of segregated public schools in the United States was unconstitutional. A legal apparatus was set in place whereby segregated school systems could be legally challenged by obtaining a federal court order directing schools districts to desegregate.

Social unrest was the main characteristic of the late fifties and early sixties. In 1955, fourteen-year-old Emmet Till from Chicago disappeared, only to reappear a few weeks later when his body was found wired to an old factory fan at the bottom of the river. Postmortem showed that he had been severely beaten and shot in the head. The perpetrators were apprehended and, because their trial was the first of many subsequent violent incidents, it brought on a lot of media attention.

A few months later, in another part of the country, an African-American woman, Rosa Parks[20], boarded a bus in Montgomery, Alabama. She was tired from standing at work all day, and her feet hurt. She sat down in an empty seat in the colored section of the bus. A sign separated the white section from the colored section. The driver reserved the right to move the sign when there were many whites standing. As the bus filled up with white people, the driver decided to move the sign back. When he asked Rosa and three other black passengers to give up their seats, Rosa refused. She was arrested. Her arrest triggered a systematic response among the civil rights community in Montgomery: a boycott of public transportation. At the head of the boycott was a young pastor of the Baptist Church on Dexter Avenue in Montgomery,

20 See appendix 2 for a short biography.

Reverend Martin Luther King, Jr. The boycott was a historical event that lasted over a year and ended on November 13, 1956 when the Supreme Court finally ruled that the Montgomery segregation law was unconstitutional.

The government rulings that were being passed did not meet with everyone's approval. Riots, dissention, hatred, and acts of violence broke out daily in every part of the country. Brown v. Board of Education sparked off tension in many places across the United States during years to come. Of special mention is Central High School in Little Rock, Arkansas. This was the school chosen by the mayor of Little Rock together with the school board to begin the implementation of the Supreme Court's ruling concerning Brown v. Board of Education and the gradual process of desegregation in schools.

An angry mob of protesters stood outside the school, barring the entrance of nine African-American students. Each day, the students were escorted in and smuggled out. The crisis escalated and created such racial antagonism between whites and blacks that by the fourth day, the nine students had to be escorted into the building by the army.

Another instance of racial tension triggered by the ruling of Brown v. Board of Education happened much later, in 1962, at the University of Mississippi. James Meredith, an African-American who applied to study at the university was rejected twice. He took the complaint to court and won the case. After much rioting and picketing from the white population, James Meredith became the first black student to be admitted at the University of Mississippi.

The 1961 Freedom Riders put to the test the recent

rulings concerning desegregation of bus terminals. There were sit-ins such as the Greensboro sit-in of 1960 in North Carolina and marches like the Selma to Montgomery Marches of 1965 in Alabama. The Civil Rights Movement, with Martin Luther King, Jr. as one of the leaders, marched into all areas of life, seeking to put an end to segregation. In 1963, King helped plan a massive march in Washington, D.C., where an estimated two hundred and fifty thousand people attended. It was here where he presented his famous speech, "I Have a Dream."

Dr. King's speeches and beliefs influenced may other groups and raised consciousness among minority groups. In turn, as society became more revolutionized, people asked for an end to inequalities in different sectors of society and for minorities to be recognized. Other groups, like the Chicano Movement, emerged.

The Chicano Movement, also known as Chicano Civil Rights Movement, Mexican American Civil Rights Movement, and *El Movimiento*, sought political empowerment and recognition within society. The movement dealt with the immediate problems confronting the Mexican-American population, especially such issues as unequal educational and employment opportunities, police brutality, and political disenfranchisement. The early heroes of the movement, Rodolfo Gonzales and Reies López Tijerina, blamed the United States for not meeting the promises made in the Treaty of Guadalupe Hidalgo and stated that Mexican Americans needed to reclaim their birthright and cultural heritage which had been stolen by the United States. They talked of a new nation, Aztlán, and had mainly students as followers. Activists formed a new group called MEChA (*Movimiento Estudiantil Chicano de Aztlán*) promoting Chicano and ethno-nationalist studies.

LGBT — Stonewall

The lesbian, gay, bi-sexual, and transgender movements played their part to influence the feminist movement to a certain extent. Although they came later, and were themselves influenced by the Civil Rights Movement, they helped shape and modify certain sectors of the feminist movement. With the increase in sexual openness and acceptance, the homosexual movement arose, becoming first, the Gay Liberation Front (GLF) and echoing the women's lib movement by "coming out" to ask for certain institutions to be abolished, while at the same time, rejecting the sexual roles imposed on homosexuals by society at large.

Homosexuality in twentieth-century America took a turn after the Second World War. In an attempt at restoring social order and shared values, anti-communistic tendencies were targeted as subversive and anti-American. Senator McCarthy funded agencies and institutions whose sole purpose was to seek out communist sympathizers from the United States government, any agency or body connected to the government, the army, and other institutions that were deemed as security risks for the nation. Not only were anti-communists targeted in this purge, but also anarchists and homosexuals— the rationale for the latter being that they could be easily blackmailed, and, therefore, were in a position of risk to themselves and to others. It is believed that between 1947 and 1950 over seven thousand people connected with the government were discharged from the military, fired from their posts, and denied a job within the government for being suspected of being a homosexual. In fact, the FBI kept lists of known homosexuals and of their contacts. At the same time, police constantly raided bars, clubs, beaches, and parks, arresting and openly denouncing the "culprits" in newspapers. University teachers and professors were targeted in a nationwide sweep, and were arrested, harassed, humiliated, and even, in some cases, claimed that homosexuals suffered from some sort of mental illness. Meanwhile, researchers dissected and studied the brains of dead men and women who had led a homosexual lifestyle and compared them to brains of heterosexual people. Not surprisingly, no differences were found. Evelyn Hooker's ground-breaking work concerning the adjustment of nonclinical homosexual men against a comparable group of heterosexual men helped homosexuality be removed from the list of mental illnesses found in the American Psychiatrist Association's manual (DSM-Diagnostic and Statistical Manual). After carrying out a one-year study with a grant from the National Institute of Mental Health, Dr. Hooker found that there was no measurable psychological difference between homosexuals and heterosexuals.

Notwithstanding these results and other similar research, social unrest bred further social unrest, and homosexuals, fearing for their lives, continued to lead double lives to avoid persecution. Though there were groups and clubs formed where homosexuals could get together and discuss their issues, get support, and generally be themselves, these groups were on the fringes and were only known to a few. As the homosexual population grew, so did the need to have safe places in which to meet. One of these was the Stonewall Inn.

The Stonewall Inn was a gay bar. They did not have a liquor license, so the owners paid off a police officer once a week, and the bar was kept free from raids. It was a safe place in which to dance and be oneself. The door was guarded, patronage was by word of mouth, they signed the book at the front, and whatever went on inside stayed inside. The club appealed to gay men, lesbians, and transvestites; they were white, black, and Latino.

Though police officers were paid off, raids did happen at times—after all, it was *the* gay bar in town. Police asked for identification during these raids, and arrested people without ID on the spot.

On June 28th 1969, four undercover police, male and female, infiltrated the establishment. They waited until their backups were outside, then they flipped on the lights and shouted "Police." The bar was packed, and in the ensuing confusion, patrons ran to the doors and to the bathroom windows to escape, creating a chaotic scene. The raid did not go as planned. Patrons who complied with the search and ID check were released, but instead of leaving, they crowded outside. The fact that they were standing there attracted passersby, and soon a huge crowd was congregated outside the bar. Patrons pushed out from the premises by the police turned to clowning and comedy, and their tomfoolery was met with cheers and applause from the ever-growing crowd.

Suddenly, someone shouted, "Gay power!"

A scuffle ensued between an officer and a transvestite. Another scuffle ended in a lesbian being clubbed over the head, and suddenly the crowd was not joking anymore. The merry singing turned to angry silence and garbage cans, bottles, trash, stones, and anything within reach was hurled at the police, who had no choice but to take refuge inside the building.

Stonewall marked a new era for homosexuals.

Major Achievements

Consciousness Raising

The new group of feminists that emerged after the war was the direct result of a post-war economic boom which set the standards for a middle-class suburban expansion. A baby boom ensued, setting up the traditional nuclear family at the core of the American value system. Capitalism was hailed as the vital model that would favor middle-class development. The media, especially television, carried overt messages of idealized domesticity placing women once again where she belonged: as mother and housewife.

At the same time that all these issues were permeating the very core of many societies around the world—especially the American society—women found their own voices in what they called "consciousness raising" groups. Men were not allowed into these groups, and women found that they could voice their opinions better and more freely without the male influence affecting their decisions. Women found that these groups gave them a common ground on which to share experiences. Issues never expressed before were openly discussed in these groups, and for many women, it was a space in which they could explore and discover ideas that would have otherwise been dampened by the male presence. It was here where many women discovered that the female "agenda" had never, in the history of humanity, been a part of the male agenda.

For some women these groups were the launching pad to challenge the status quo. For others, these gatherings were a source of conflict. A new, younger generation of feminists emerged with different views than the older generations, and they strived forward with their own agendas. This group of young feminists clashed painfully with older ones in an upheaval of social values that, in their view, were antiquated and, frankly, they did not care for anymore. This new, over-zealous generation with their "correct views" may have lacked the experience of the older generation, but they certainly did not lack the courage and power to push on forward.

Personal is Political

Second wave feminism encouraged women to question the status quo and to look at women's lives to understand how deeply politicized their personal lives were. "Personal is political" became a household phrase, symbolizing the need for women to demand an equal footing in society and to demand an end to women's oppression and discrimination.

It was at this boiling point of social unrest that Betty Friedan's best seller, *The Feminine Mystique*, hit the streets. It was 1963, and the book became a milestone in the history of the movement. Friedan's book was a great success by the mere fact that it represented the voices of real-life women speaking out from every page. Women were ready to listen, and women identified themselves and their struggles in every sentence in the book. Though the book appealed mainly to women of middle and upper classes of the (mainly) white population, it also touched upon the lives of all women, regardless of color, social standing, or creed. *The Feminine Mystique* was what women had been waiting for. It challenged, among other things, the ideology of female domesticity.

As the American society became more affluent, consumerism fueled the idea that more comforts could be obtained with a second income. Women saw this as their opportunity to become further educated, and millions of married women entered the job market.

Margaret Sanger, a nurse in New York City, had witnessed many women die from childbirth and self-induced abortion. In the early 1900s, she set up the first clinic promoting birth control for women, and she envisioned that one day a birth control pill would exist that would be an alternative to the diaphragm. In the 1950s, Margaret and a colleague, Katherine McCormick, met with Dr. Gregory Goodwin Pincus, an endocrinologist and researcher. The two women outlined their idea, and he set to work on it. The idea was an oral contraceptive for women: the pill. Although there were political glitches along the way, the pill came into existence and was finally approved by the FDA (Food and Drug Administration) in 1960. By 1963, over one million women were using it.

Thanks to Sanger and McCormick, women now had some sort of reproductive control (though not complete control of their bodies), giving them the choice of if and when to enlarge their families and, on the flip side, to decide if and when to enter the workforce. Of course, as more and more women began to work outside of their homes, more and more of them discovered and resented the truth about work discrimination and unequal pay between the genders, about which, for the most part, they could not even complain, let alone change the situation.

Two years earlier, in 1961, the Commission on the Status of Women was established by the Kennedy administration to explore issues pertaining to women and, at the same time, to make recommendations concerning policies with regards to employment, education, tax laws, and social security. At the head of the commission was Mrs. Eleanor Roosevelt. The idea behind the Commission was to try to find suitable compromises between organized labor laws and feminists who argued for the protection of women workers against labor exploitation among other issues. Women entering the workforce were a source of disagreement for the population at large as many men and women rejected the idea. For traditional minds, the notion of women working outside of the home contradicted the deep-rooted values of a woman's role within the family: that of raising a healthy family and, therefore, contributing to society by being a pillar of rectitude in the heart of her community. Still, the Kennedy administration saw the need to resolve these issues through the creation of the Commission. Some scholars and investigators have since argued that Kennedy's move was purely political and did not have women's issues at heart. Kennedy saw the need to have women in the workplace in order to increase the workforce in his desire to compete with Russia in the space and arms race.

Regardless of intent, the results found by the commission in 1963 were astounding. The report, called the Peterson Report (after Esther Peterson who headed the Department of Labor's Women's Bureau), found that virtually every area of the American woman's life was discriminated upon. Though it proposed a number of initiatives such as child care for working mothers, equal employment opportunities, paid maternity leave, and others, the report did not mention an Equal Rights Amendment (ERA). Although the majority of the population thought the ERA was a positive move for women, many women (and men) opposed it. They thought that the ERA would open the doors to such issues as men abandoning their families, gay marriages, women in the military, and other controversial topics. Ironically, repeated rejection made the ERA a rallying point for women of diverse backgrounds to band together and draw national attention to the impending need for the amendment. Just like the first wave had had a common cause, so did, now, this second wave.

Armed with *The Feminine Mystique* and drawing strength and tactical maneuvering from the civil rights movement, a second wave of feminists rose to meet the challenges. Many women found that their efforts were opposed by both men and women. The outcome was more women forming more grassroots groups and more liberation organizations that continued to address new issues.

The fighting paid off. The women's movement won a great victory: the Equal Pay Act (EPA) of 1963. The Equal Pay Act of 1963 is a federal law amending the Fair Labor Standards Act. The aim of the EPA was to abolish the existing disparity in wages between the sexes. President Kennedy signed the act into law. Congress declared that industries had to comply to the new law for the following reason:

- Sex discrimination depresses wages and living standards for employees necessary for their health and efficiency;
- Sex discrimination prevents the maximum utilization of the available labor resources;
- Sex discrimination tends to cause labor disputes, thereby burdening, affecting, and obstructing commerce;
- Sex discrimination burdens commerce and the free flow of goods in commerce; and
- Sex discrimination constitutes an unfair method of competition.

Under Section 206 (Minimum Wage) of title 29 of the U.S. Code, the law provides that:

> No employer having employees subject to any provisions of this section shall discriminate, within any establishment in which such employees are employed, between employees on the basis of sex by paying wages to employees in such establishment at a rate less than the rate at which he pays wages to employees of the opposite sex in such establishment for equal work on jobs the performance of which requires equal skill, effort, and responsibility, and which are performed under similar working conditions, except where such payment is made pursuant to (i) a seniority system; (ii) a merit system; (iii) a system which measures earnings by quantity or quality of production; or (iv) a differential based on any other factor other than sex.[21]

21 Taken from the US Equal Employment Opportunity Commission in: http://www.eeoc.gov/laws/statutes/epa.cfm

This was a major achievement for women. In 1963, women earned less than sixty percent of men's salaries in the same post and with the same credentials. Though today, according to the Board of Labor Statistics, women's salaries have risen and the gap between male and female salaries has narrowed, women still earn at least ten percent less than their male counterparts. In 2005, Senator Hillary Rodham Clinton introduced the Paycheck Fairness Act which proposed to amend the EPA's fourth affirmative defense; and in 2009, President Barack Obama introduced the Lilly Ledbetter Fair Pay Act, which made gender unequal paychecks a violation of the law.

Another major achievement for women happened the following year, 1964. Title VII of the Civil Rights Act was enacted. Title VII prohibits discrimination on the basis of race, color, religion, and national origin. It also prohibits discrimination against an individual because of his/her association with another individual of a particular race, color, religion, sex, and national origin. Also, an employer cannot discriminate against a person because of interracial marriage.

The stage was set. Many women, in fighting sexism, found inspiration in the lives of black women in the Civil Rights Movement who broke with sexual stereotypes and became the first to express criticisms and sexist practices.

By 1965, black militancy had become the motivating factor of the Civil Rights Movement, but white women were not welcome. Black feminists argued that class oppression, sexism, and racism were intertwined, and even though black women faced the same struggles as white women, they had to contend, not only with the issue of inequality (i.e. sexism), but with the issue of diversity (i.e. racism) as well.

At the same time that Title VII was passed, the Equal Employment Opportunity Commission (EEOC) was established to enforce federal laws that prohibited job discrimination, to uphold the newly signed Title VII, to investigate complaints against sexual discrimination, and to advocate for employees who had faced sexual discrimination among others.

As is usually the case with new laws, the wheels of bureaucracy do not turn fast enough, and red tape contributes to the overall snail's pace of social change and adjustment. Therefore, angered by the EEOC's failure to enforce the anti-discrimination provision of Title VII, a group of women formed in 1966 a much needed official group to represent and campaign for women's concerns. It was the National Organization for Women (NOW). The group was modeled after the very successful NAACP (National Association for the Advancement of Colored People), and the main issue at the core of NOW was to be the watchdog for women of all races. At the helm of NOW were women like Betty Friedan, Shirley Chisholm, Gloria Steinem, and others who pressured politicians into becoming aware of the plights of women, urging them to take action against inequalities and injustices in order to improve the quality of women's lives. Though NOW appealed mainly to educated, middle-class white women, it did have its share of diversity; and over the years, the membership of NOW has increased dramatically to become more heterogeneous.

NOW appealed to women of all races and classes for a number of reasons, at the forefront of which was the fact that this newly formed group did not seek to challenge subordination in domestic life but, rather, it fought for women's integration into the working sphere. Another important reason that banded this diverse group of women was the fact that NOW took a stronger political stance and it supported more daring and controversial issues such as lesbian and gay rights, abortion, and others. But no matter how many issues they supported, the ERA was never lost from sight and was constantly being pushed forward time and again.

Groups of women sprouted overnight, each of which dealt with different issues that ranged from reproductive rights to equal pay to contraception to divorce to common property to poverty to childcare, and a thousand other issues women felt compelled to speak out for. Each group, advocating for their own agendas, clamored for political and legal support, and each group maintained a high profile in the media.

The New Left, a group that did not support the left ideology of Russia or Trotsky, but rather, was more liberal and radical in its political thinking, drew the attention of students and academia, both male and female, more than it did any other sector of the population. These activists rejected authoritarianism, unchecked affluence, and many others "isms" associated with the emergent capitalistic ideology in society. The New Left focused mainly on more personalized issues such as anarchism. Society was viewed as The Establishment, and advocates of the New Left were anti-Establishment. They were socialist in their philosophy, influenced by the Vietnam War and Chinese Cultural Revolution, upholding such personalities as Mao Zedong and Fidel Castro as key contributors to this new ideology. Needless to say, some feminist groups took on a leftist stance, while others rejected it.

Another group of women that emerged from within the liberal feminist and working class feminist discussion groups were radical feminists. This new group was made up of younger women that perceived failings in the New Left, in liberal feminism, and above all, in NOW—a group which, they thought, ignored the effects of women's subordination in the family. They also accused NOW that by not taking a stronger stance against subordination, women were integrated into a class and race stratified system.

The radical feminists' point of view was very different from that of NOW, and their main focus was aimed at dismantling this system of class and race stratification that invariably managed to place women at the bottom of the ladder. Central to the radical feminist philosophy is the notion that patriarchal societies breed inequality between men and women; and more specifically, they believe that in patriarchal societies men dominate women. To the radical feminist, patriarchy divides rights, privileges, and power along gender lines, making the male dominant over an oppressed female. Being more militant in their approach, radical feminists oppose the political and social organization of societies—constructs which are in place due to the fact that a patriarchal system is in place. It was this group of feminists who introduced the notion of "consciousness raising" groups (though many other groups soon adopted the practice), and it was Carol Hanisch, at the forefront of a radical group of feminists, who coined "the personal is political."

All in all, as far as every feminist group was concerned, conventional norms of femininity needed to be challenged, as was the case in 1968 when the Miss America pageant became the focus of the radical feminist group, the Redstockings. Theirs was a protest against a patriarchal society's view of the female body. The idea stemmed from the fact that, in those contests, women are judged like cattle; the contests are degrading and mindless; they see women as "boob-girlie" symbols, and all women are judged on how their looks please men rather than on their value as human beings.

For the event, through a press release, the Redstockings invited every conceivable group of women (college women, black women, pro-birth control groups, pro-abortion groups, peace groups, and hundreds more) they could think of to attend the day-long event on the boardwalk in front of Atlantic City's Convention Hall where the pageant was taking place. Women came from Canada and from as far as Florida and the West Coast, and there, on the boardwalk, the protesters performed a skit outside the hall in which they crowned a sheep "Miss America." They also set up a Freedom Trash Can where women were invited to throw in any object they deemed oppressing. In went a whole range of objects that included: dishcloths, *Playboy* magazines, false eyelashes, high heels, girdles, wigs, *Cosmopolitan* magazines, and thousands of other articles, among them the famous bras from which the myth was born. The following day, the newspapers called the women "bra burners," and even though the Freedom Trash Can was never set on fire, the myth has persisted.

Aside from the Freedom Trash Can and crowning the sheep, they protested other points which included: the degrading and mindless girlie symbols, racism (since its beginning in 1921, Miss America had never had a black finalist. In fact, it was not until 1984 that Vanessa Williams became the first black Miss America), promotion of consumerism, promotion of undesirable traits for women (sexy yet innocent, young, delicate yet coping, apolitical, of a certain height and weight, among others), devaluation of women's intelligence (men are judged by their actions and women by their beauty), and oppression of women through male-created standards.

The banners these women held read: NO MORE MISS AMERICA.

As the '60s rolled into the '70s, women's publications increased at tremendous speed. By 1975 there were over a hundred women's liberation journals, newspapers, and magazines. Among them were such ground-breaking books as Germaine Greer's *Female Eunuch* (1970) in which she argued that women did not realize how much men hated them, and how much women were taught to hate themselves.

Another publication that set a milestone was *Ms Magazine* (1971), co-founded by Gloria Steinem, and which became an instant success. It came out first as a "sample" because it was predicted to be a flop. However, it proved everybody wrong by selling over a quarter of a million copies in one week. It was a raving success. The title "Ms" gave women a rightful place, neither owned by their fathers nor owned by their husbands. Whereas for men "Mr." gave no indication of their marital status, there was not an equivalent for women. At a stage in which many women did not want to be defined according to their marital status, and many were keeping their last names after marriage, the title "Ms" was a great success and was quickly adopted into mainstream society.

Society was revolutionized. It was experiencing a change and women were leading the change. As feminism gained impetus in every sphere, women expressed themselves more openly and with more aplomb.

In the sports sector, Bobby Riggs, a number one tennis champion for three years, challenged and defeated Margaret Court in a tennis match in which he declared that men were superior to women. He then went on to call Billie Jean King to the "battle of the sexes" tennis match. After some consideration, King accepted the challenge, and on September 20, 1973 with an approximate fifty million spectators worldwide, King defeated Riggs in three straight sets. Needless to say, it was a victory for feminists everywhere—men were definitely not superior to women.

In the political sector, feminists were making waves too. Shirley Chisholm, in 1968, became the first African-American woman elected to Congress. She did not stop there, by all means. Having represented New York's 12th Congressional District, in 1972, she became the first major-party black candidate for President of the United States. She was also the first woman to run for the Democratic presidential nomination.

In the educational sector, a new program of study was making its appearance through student and faculty activism. The first Women's Studies Program was finally off the ground after much rallying and petitioning at San Diego State College (now San Diego State University) in 1970. Soon, other universities followed suit. Today, there are more than seven hundred institutions offering women's studies and gender studies at undergraduate and post-graduate levels in the United States alone.

Other Major Achievements

1970	In the case Schultz vs. Wheaton Glass Co. it was ruled by the court that an employer cannot change the job titles of female workers so that the company pays them differently. This practice fell under the protection of the Equal Pay Act.
1972	Title IX of the Education Amendment banned sex discrimination in schools. According to the United States Code Section 20: "No person in the United States shall, on the basis of sex, be excluded from participation in, be denied the benefits of, or be subjected to discrimination under any education program or activity receiving Federal financial assistance." This ruling has led to an increase of female enrollment in schools and colleges.
1972	In Eisenstadt vs. Baird the Supreme Court established the right for unmarried persons to use contraceptives on the same basis as married couples.
1973	The EEOC upheld the 1968 rule whereby sex-segregated help wanted ads in newspapers were illegal. This opened the way for women to apply for higher-paying jobs which up until then had been reserved only for men.

1973	Roe vs. Wade shocked the nation when the Supreme Court established the right for a woman to have a safe and legal abortion. The ruling basically gave the woman the right, with her doctor, to choose to terminate the pregnancy without restrictions and with a complete right to privacy. The ruling was based on the fact that the Texas law violated the constitutional rights (Ninth Amendment of the U.S. Constitution) of Ms. Roe and other women.
1976	The first marital rape law ever passed by Congress was repealed. The law was an age-old ruling based on the idea that said " . . .the husband cannot be guilty of a rape committed by himself upon his lawful wife, for by their mutual matrimonial consent and contract, the wife hath given herself in kind unto the husband which she cannot retract."[1] Although today all fifty states consider marital rape a crime, not all of them consider it as serious as stranger rape.
1978	The Pregnancy Discrimination Act was enacted in which it became illegal for a woman to be discriminated upon, fired, or denied a job or promotion because she was pregnant. The Act also states that a pregnant woman cannot be forced to take pregnancy leave if she is still willing and capable of working.

Year after year the battle was kept up, and year after year women were able to make a difference in their lives, pushing forward inch by inch. In the midst of this, women's fashion took on a style of its own to reflect the new woman of the decade. The wide shoulder pads told the story of a successful career woman "power dressing" to compete in the business world of men. Besides that, shoulder pads improved the postural imperfections and highlighted cleaner, straighter lines that made women look more gracious and "business-like."

Finally, the second wave rolled into the '80s and, as was to be expected, there were as many discontented people as there were happy ones. A backlash within the feminist ranks and from anti-feminist groups became more prominent as time wore on and achievements continued. Despite the fact that the movement had branched into liberal feminists (who focused on women's rights as individuals), radical feminists (who fought against a patriarchal society), lesbians (who, though feminists, aligned themselves with the gay movement), African-American feminists (who did not see themselves a part of the white, middle-class feminists), Latina feminists (who also felt that their needs were not being addressed by mainstream feminism), and many others, each of these groups held the ERA as their common cause, though all of them had separate agendas of their own. Once again, the ERA was introduced, and once again it was publicly rejected, this time by President Ronald Reagan.

Nevertheless, women pressed on, urging legislators to address such women's issues as rape (how victims were handled in courts), sexual harassment, pay equity, affirmative action, and reproductive rights, among others.

For many women, the rejection of the ERA in 1982 was a major blow, but for other women it was not. Many feminists took comfort in the fact that by now, social attitude toward women had changed, and it was only a matter of time before the ERA was ratified. With their victories so far, feminists helped educate women, the result of which was three-pronged. First of all, by insisting on educating women, women were able to see and understand their personal lives as second class to men. Secondly, education led women into posts that allowed them to pressure the system into making changes for the benefit of women. Thirdly, because women of different ethnic backgrounds, social class, and sexual preferences were more prominent in the public eye, feminists were in a position to prove the idea that "women" could not be classified in the false images upheld by society, nor could "women" be expected to continue to play a role predetermined by society. "Women" were too diverse to be lumped into one category.

Debates around the Equal Rights Amendment (ERA)

The Equal Rights Amendment states:

- Section 1. Equality of rights under the law shall not be denied or abridged by the United States or by any state on account of sex.
- Section 2. The Congress shall have the power to enforce, by appropriate legislation, the provisions of this article.
- Section 3. This amendment shall take effect two years after the date of ratification.

The Equal Rights Amendment was a proposed amendment to the United States Constitution. It was introduced for the first time into Congress in 1923 and, under this law, it would guarantee equality for women. Historically, the Thirteenth Amendment did away with slavery, the Fourteenth Amendment declared that "all persons born or naturalized in the

United States" were citizens and therefore guaranteed equal protection of the laws. However, in referring to the electorate, the word "male" was introduced into the Constitution for the first time, thereby protecting only men's rights. The Fifteenth Amendment guaranteed citizens the right to vote regardless of race, color, or previous condition of servitude, however, women were denied the ballot.

When the Nineteenth Amendment was ratified in 1920, it gave women, specifically, the right to vote. However, the Fourteenth Amendment needed to be changed. This led to Alice Paul to write the Lucretia Mott Amendment, which was introduced annually in Congress until it passed in reworded form in 1972. The Lucretia Mott Amendment stated that: "Men and women shall have equal rights throughout the United States and every place subject to its jurisdiction."

Therefore, in 1943, reflecting the Fifteenth and Nineteenth Amendments, Alice Paul took upon herself to rewrite the Lucretia Mott Amendment (now called the Alice Paul Amendment) to read: "Equality of rights under the law shall not be denied or abridged by the United States or by any state on account of sex."

Though the ERA passed the U.S. Senate and House of Representatives in 1972, Congress included a seven-year ratification deadline and in which thirty-eight out of fifty states (three-fourths) had to ratify. The seven-year deadline came and went with only thirty-five states ratifying it, and so Congress extended the deadline to 1982. Yet, despite demonstrations, marches, hunger strikes, and civil disobedience, the Republican Party struck it off their platform to concentrate on other issues.

Interestingly enough, the Equal Rights Amendment has been (and still is) a source of contention and heated debate for women. When the ERA was presented, the amendment promised that it would benefit women by elevating them out of their second-class status. The truth of matter was that, even as far back as 1964, as the United States Constitution stood then, women already enjoyed every constitutional right that men enjoyed. In other words, the ERA would not end discrimination against them.

The reality concerning this most heated issue is that the proposers of ERA could not show anything positive that would benefit women, yet those opposing it (both men and women) argued that the ERA would cause more harm than good. The argument the opposers held on to was the fact that if things were to be taken to an extreme, the ERA could potentially take away legal rights that women already possessed. Some areas exposed were, for example:

- Having the same rights as men would mean mothers, wives, and widows could lose traditional benefits. In such areas as marriage, property laws, divorce, child custody, alimony, and so forth, women would lose out.
- Privacy would be invaded by federal courts who would now decide on the definitions of the words "sex" (as in male/female or heterosexual/homosexual) and "equality or rights" within the ERA.
- The ERA allowed for homosexual rights and homosexual marriages to be commonplace; there would be homosexual laws which, in turn, would affect many other areas of society.
- ERA would take away rights from women students as well as impacting other areas of society—the worst

impact of all being on the personal sphere. Besides this, ERA would force all colleges, universities, and other educational bodies to be fully co-educational which, in turn, would render Title IX unconstitutional. There would be no more single-sex schools/ programs and such bodies as Boys Scouts, Girl Scouts, YWCA, and YMCA would suffer in the process.

- With the ratification of ERA, women would have to serve in the army when the country decided and so they would lose their traditional exemption from conscription at the age of eighteen.

- With ERA in place, abortion rights would be in the hands of the United States Constitution and by implication make abortion funding a constitutional right. This, in the eyes of pro-life advocates would be a justification to rampant abortion.

- ERA would demand "unisex" insurance. This means that, at the moment, women exercise a right to be charged lower rates by insurance companies in the areas of life and automobile accidents. This is because statistically women live longer than men and women drivers have fewer accidents. The ERA would demand that women pay higher insurance rates—a very peculiar "right" to demand.

- And countless others.

The fight still continues to have the ERA ratified. There is a legal argument that maintains that although it has been a long time with several time extensions, the original thirty-five states that ratified are still valid. This means that only three more states would be needed to pass it. Since the 1970s, five of those states (Idaho, Kentucky, Nebraska, Tennessee, and South Dakota) have rescinded their ratifications for different reasons. Whether this is legitimate or not remains to be seen.

THIRD WAVE FEMINISM

The '90s and Beyond

The '80s eased into the '90s and a legacy was left in the hands of the new generations whose roots were firmly planted in the second wave. Consciousness raising groups and writings were in place, and feminist thought was encouraged more than ever. Women activists continued to raise new issues that altered women's lives and the way they saw themselves and how society treated them. "Old" issues like birth control and reproductive rights, sexism, domestic violence, and sexual discrimination were maintained at the forefront, and "new" issues like rape, battery, child pornography, and others were being addressed using the power of the media, the courts, and legislature.

Women had made a breakthrough in education, the military, healthcare, sports, the workplace, and home life, and now they had to face the backlash that originated from all those areas in which they had gained so much ground. In short, by the end of the decade of the '80s, the women's movement had revolutionized society, and they had succeeded in revolutionizing the mind of the American population. Indeed, as many countries have become accepting of these changes and principles, some of the issues are no longer seen as solely a feminist concern because they have been absorbed by mainstream society and now have become part of the system. For example, nobody in Western countries would ever question women their right to vote, nobody would ever question a woman's desire to be educated, and most certainly, nobody would question her decision to seek work in accordance with her chosen education.

The second wave of feminists succeeded in such achievements as more equitable wages, the right to initiate a divorce, the right to make decisions involving women's own bodies, and many other issues. Whether the battle has been won or not remains as the next question, for indeed, some feminists would argue that all that needs to be done is to maintain that which has been achieved, while others would argue that there are still many more milestones to overcome. Besides, as with many ideologies, factions tend to appear, and before long, the stronger (in terms of followers, convictions, and more likely to make an impact on society) of these new groups will shoot forward with a different agenda. And the feminist movement is no exception.

The question whether the offshoot that stemmed from the feminist movement in the '90s is in fact a *third* wave or not is an arguable point.

One argument for pro-wave feminists is that the term "wave" denotes a moment in history (spanning several years) when women had a common issue that needed attention and needed to be resolved. The first wave sought to gain the right to vote. Along the way, women met, discussed, and found other concerns and questions that needed to be resolved too, and they set out to do so. But after their victory with the Nineteenth Amendment, the feminist movement became more home centered and quietly continued to chip away at the more traditional aspects of society so that women could continue to change their lives for the better.

This same group of feminists would argue that the second wave showed similar characteristics. Once again an issue needed attention and needed to be resolved, and once again, women *en masse* set out to make the change. At the forefront of their agenda, this time, was the inclusion of women in traditionally male-dominated areas. Because of historical circumstances, once again, just like in the first wave, there was a need for women to unite into a forceful front in order to change the status quo for the benefit of women. And just like the first wave, it marked a moment in history in which feminism was at the forefront of every newspaper and every medium of communication.

Opposing the pro-wavers are those who do not believe in waves per se, but rather see feminism as a continuum with its beginning in the nineteenth century. They also argue that the third wave is simply a continuation (or offshoot) from the second. Rebecca Walker (daughter of novelist Alice Walker) is said to have been the originator of this new group of feminists.

Historically speaking, the fact that in some decades feminism has not had as much media attention as in others does not mean that there is not a new generation of feminists seeking to challenge and wishing to expand from where the last generation (the second wave) left off.

Realizing that the group of feminists her mother had belonged to had achieved important gains for women, Rebecca Walker took the stance that a new direction was necessary to take the second wave into the '90s and beyond. It was an obvious response to the realization that women were made up of "many colors, ethnicities, nationalities, religions, and cultural backgrounds."[22] In short, this new wave of feminism would embrace diversity and change. As a contributor editor to *Ms Magazine*, Rebecca Walker confirmed the birth of the third wave when she wrote an article entitled "Becoming the Third Wave" in response to the 1991 Anita Hill and Clarence Thomas case in which Hill accused Thomas (a man nominated to the United Supreme Court) of sexual harassment. Hill lost the case. In her article, Rebecca Walker stated, "I am not a post-feminism feminist. I am the third-wave."[23]

This third wave of feminists who took over from the last goes beyond the accomplishment of the last generation and questions new issues such as gender and sexuality. The third wave includes queer theory, women of color consciousness, critical theory, post-structuralism, and many other issues while, at the same time, deemphasizing the overthrowing of a perceived oppression of a patriarchal society by emphasizing equality between the sexes.

For the third wave, equality has not been achieved, and that's why feminism cannot be seen as a wave but rather a continuation of the movement in a different direction which will address new issues as they surface. Third wave feminists also argue that equality is not just the right to sexual or gender expression, but rather, real equality will be achieved when women can reclaim the right to make choices in *all* areas of life.

22 Tong, Rosemarie (2009). *Feminist Thought: A More Comprehensive Introduction* (3 ed.). Westview Press (Perseus Books). pp. 284–285.
23 Walker, Rebecca, "Becoming the Third Wave" in *Ms. Magazine* (January/February, 1992) pp. 39–41

Having said this, third wave feminists have also put themselves in a situation that may perhaps disfavor them. By the mere fact that they have attempted to address such issues as gender, sexuality, and even feminism itself, they have trapped themselves in the limitations of definitions. Definitions are limiting. In fact, some third wave feminists shy away from the word "feminist" due to the inevitable pitfalls of interpretation. They believe that the word "feminism" may be misinterpreted as insensitive to the notion of gender, gender roles, and their fluid nature.

Third Wave Agenda

Be it what it may, a new—for the sake of this book, third wave—group of feminists exists whose agenda is different from that of the last wave. Third wave feminism urges the young woman of today to become involved in those social issues that affect them, issues like reproductive health, reproductive freedom, class, and others. In the same way that second wave feminists employed consciousness-raising groups to make women aware of issues pertaining to them and address those issues accordingly, these younger feminists also make use of resources present in modern-day society such as making use of networking across professional organizations and urging women to be more active in public education.

In this group of feminists, there are many great and audacious women who have made important contributions in the expounding of thoughts and theories. Rebecca Walker, at the forefront, also co-established the Third Wave Direct Action

Corporation that works to promote activist strategies and leadership ideas to aid women. Rebecca Walker has also written extensively on race, gender politics, and feminism.

Another important figure is Naomi Wolf who has tutored and spoken to audiences on topics of social justice, gender equality, ethics, and empowerment of women leaders among others. She continues to be actively involved in women's issues and is co-founder of the American Freedom Campaign whose mission is the defense of the Constitution.

Wolf's most famous book is *The Beauty Myth*, which was published in 1990. In it, she argues that beauty is a social construct determined by patriarchal societies with the intent of maintaining its own hegemony. At the same time, women are punished physically and psychologically when they fail to achieve and conform to those patriarchal social constructs. Another important feminist of the third wave is bell hooks (Gloria Jean Watkins), who has written extensively in the areas of race, class, and gender, and how these three issues produce and perpetuate systems of domination and oppression. One of her more famous books, *Ain't I a Woman*, examines the historical impact of racism and sexism on black women, the devaluation of black womanhood, the notion of a patriarchy made up of white supremacist capitalists, the marginalization of black women, and how feminism has ignored race and class.

The core of third wave feminism is the idea of gendered oppression and how it is interconnected with other forms of discrimination such as race, sexual orientation, and class. Third wave feminism has made a point of making transgender issues part of their agenda (as opposed to their being rejected by second wave feminists who saw non-heterosexual women as an embarrassment to the movement). Another area of achievement is their reaching out to women of other nations (mainly in the developing world), thus creating a global view of feminism and drawing strength from each other in the hope of eradicating all forms of discrimination in all cultures across the world.

The '90s was a decade of great importance in the feminist battle against discrimination. For a start, 1992 was an election year in the United States. Appalled by the all-male panel of senators, more than sixty million women voted that year in the presidential elections, helping to elect twenty-four new women to the House and five to the Senate. The following year, 1993, saw the first female United States Attorney General (Janet Wood Reno) and also saw the second woman on the Supreme Court (Ruth Bader Ginsburg); 1996 saw the first female Secretary of State (Madeleine Albright) and, for the first time in United States history, the First Lady (Hillary Rodham Clinton) had an independent political, legal, activist, and public service career.

In the sports sector, in the 1996 Summer Olympics, U.S. women took home nineteen gold medals, ten silver, and nine bronze. This was seen as a result of Title IX which allowed large numbers of women and girls to become actively engaged in sports.

As to religion, by 1996 also, there were an unprecedented number of female bishops, priests, ministers, and rabbis.

As the '90s made their way into the new millennium, new issues arose which became prominent on the third wave agenda.

Reproductive rights

Reproductive rights have always been one of the main concerns of feminism, especially with the second wave. On January 22, 1973, feminism found itself taking a giant step forward in the realm of reproductive rights. It was the date in which the U.S. Supreme Court made its decision on the Roe v. Wade case and which set a precedent for all abortion cases that inevitably followed. This decision clearly recognized the right of a woman to decide whether or not to terminate her pregnancy. In short, the Court's decision gave women reproductive choices. For feminists, this moment in time marked an era in which, hopefully, women would at last come out of their second-class citizenship status every time they got pregnant. In other words, women would no longer be forced into being second class due to their pregnancies and the roles destined for them if so—housewife, mother in poverty because of her pregnancy, single mother, or any other typecast.

For the feminists of today, access to contraception is just as important as abortion. Abortion is a very controversial issue because there are emotions and sentiments attached. However, it can be argued that abortion is a necessity for many millions of women under certain circumstances. For example, when the pregnancy puts the woman's health at risk; or because the woman and her partner may not be able to support the child given their present economic conditions and, therefore, not being able to provide the child with a future; or even because the pregnancy was due to rape.

Because abortion is such an emotionally charged topic, and many advocates are against the practice, much research has been conducted with interesting results that irrevocably show that unless the woman is under excessive strain (physical, emotional, economic, psychological) she will not have an abortion for the sake of having it. It is only when a woman finds herself under duress that she will have her pregnancy terminated. For this reason, feminism believes in giving a woman the legal right to make her decision safely without being subjected to social, medical, and psychological pressures.

Sexual violence against women

Take Back the Night is the response to a social malaise that has, for a long time, been avoided or not been given the sufficient amount of importance by local authorities. Violence against women regardless of her age occurs every day in every town and every country in the world. Because of its nature, it is difficult to address efficiently and much controversy surrounds the topic. However, more could be done by authorities.

The eradication of sexual violence against women was also on the agenda of the second wave of feminists. The '70s saw the first groups of people organizing themselves and going out into the streets carrying candles in an attempt at drawing the attention of the media and of the local authorities. Yet again, another woman had been the victim of a sexual crime. Whether the woman was raped or murdered, something had to be done. People in the community had had enough. All over the world people were copying each other in an attempt at doing more than what was currently being done. In Philadelphia, in Belgium, and in Rome, groups of women and men organized marches in which thousands of people joined to protest the right of every woman (and man) to walk down the streets at night without having to fear for her life.

The most well-known case of violence against women and, at the same time least documented, is that of Jack the Ripper. It is not known who this man was, though through the evidence gathered, and the fact that he used a sharp knife or surgical instrument to kill his victims, some authorities suggest that he may have been a butcher, while other authorities suggest he may have been a surgeon or at least practiced in the medical field. Under cover of the fog that rose from the River Thames in London, Jack the Ripper would go out at night and choose his female victim. Because of the nature of his crime, "respectable" women observed a "curfew" and were indoors as soon as night time fell. However, for those women whose livelihood depended on the nature of their profession, they had no choice but to risk their lives on a lonely street corner waiting for a customer. Or for their untimely death.

It is said that Jack the Ripper murdered at least five women, though there are another six (making a total of eleven) who were slaughtered roughly in the same manner, but the evidence was not conclusive in those cases. The fact that the victims were prostitutes may have been one of the reasons why the police did not pursue the matter in greater depth. The fact that the killings stopped as suddenly as they had begun led some to believe that Jack the Ripper had met his own fate, though, to this date, nobody knows how or when.

The world over has groups reclaiming the night. In some parts of the globe the groups are called Reclaim the Night, originating from Rome (Italy) in 1976, when it was publicly disclosed that there had been over sixteen thousand rapes that year alone. Inflamed, the inhabitants marched the streets seeking international interest. Today, over thirty years later, women (and men) continue to stand up and speak out against sexual violence, especially against women. Though there is yet too much still to accomplish, Take Back the Night and Reclaim the Night have placed sexual violence in the social limelight, and they are the hope of many millions of women affected by crimes of sexual violence.

Besides this, third wave feminism has continued to increase pressure for an end to violence against women and to have stricter sanctions against the perpetrators. A brief timeline shows some of the most notable achievements in the area:

1991	A National study showed that one out of seven wives reported being raped by their husband; and in two-thirds of the rapes, they occurred more than once.
1992	The U.S. Surgeon General ranked abuse by husbands to be the leading cause of injuries to women between the ages of fifteen and forty-five. Due to this, the American Medical Association suggests that doctors screen women for signs of domestic violence.
1993	Due to joint efforts from women around the world, the United Nations began to recognize domestic violence as an international human rights concern and has since issued a Declaration on the Elimination of Violence Against Women.

1994	Congress adopted the Gender Equity in Education Act. Under this Act teachers are to be trained in gender equity, schools must promote math and science learning by girls, schools must counsel pregnant teens, and there should be overall prevention of sexual harassment.
1994	The Violence Against Women Act (VAWA) was enacted. It provides funds and services for victims of rape and domestic violence, it allows women to seek civil rights remedies for gender-related crimes, and it provides training to increase police and court officials' sensitivity. The Act also funds a national twenty-four-hour hotline for battered women. At the same time, the VAWA tightens federal penalties for sex offenders.
1998	In an EEOC lawsuit contending that hundreds of women were sexually harassed, Mitsubishi Motor Manufacturing of America paid a $34 million settlement.
1999	In New York State, a law was passed making stalking a felony.
2000	There was an EEOC lawsuit against CBS Broadcasting for sex discrimination on behalf of two-hundred women. They paid eight million dollars to settle it.
2000	In United States vs Morrison 529 U.S. 598, the Supreme Court invalidated some parts of the VAWA of 1994, stating they were unconstitutional. At the same time, the ruling permits the victims of sexual abuse to sue their attackers in federal court.
2000	The Sexual Assault Reform Act (SARA) was passed in New York State enacting changes in sexual assault and child sexual abuse laws.

| 2003 | According to the Federal Bureau of Investigation (Uniform Crime Reports of the U.S.) between the months of January and June, 30 percent of all female murder victims in the U.S. were slain by their husbands or boyfriends. |
| 2011 | Currently, Walmart is being sued for sexual discrimination concerning equal pay between sexes, promotional opportunities, and a host of other issues that favor men over women. This lawsuit could potentially run into billions of dollars and be the largest discrimination lawsuit in U.S. history yet. |

Clearly, from the feminist point of view, the war against sexual violence has not ended.

Defining Terms and Reclaiming Words

For as many words as are created or redefined in our societies, so do many others fall out of use and change over time. Changes in thinking and attitudes are constantly happening in our societies, especially in the areas of sexual and gender identity. The third wave feminist agenda has been more all-embracing and tolerant of women of different sexual preferences, gender identities, and walks of life. In an attempt at introducing vocabulary that is non-discriminating, yet informative for the non feminist or for the heterosexual person, third wave feminism has tried to define certain words and concepts with the understanding that these words are not standardized throughout society, and may be used differently by different people in different places or regions. According to third wave feminism, the terms "sex," "gender," and "sex/gender role" are separate and distinct from each other, however, for many people in society they may be one and the same, or they may be seen to overlap to the point of being almost one and the same.

In accepting these definitions, there is the assumption that there are only two of each of these terms—that is, there are only *two* sexes (male/female), *two* genders (masculine/feminine), and *two* sex/gender roles (male/female). This is not so for third wave feminism.

Third wave feminism expounds that gender identity refers to how a person identifies her/himself and has nothing to do with biological makeup since a person may identify her/himself as female, male, both, in between (third gender) or neither (agendered).

Sexual identity refers to a person's consideration of her/himself in terms of sexual/romantic attraction toward others (homosexual, heterosexual, bisexual, asexual). Once again, society has come up with its own definitions of romantic/sexual attachments following prescribed norms which, for the most part, are heterosexual in nature. Non-conformists to these rules (that is, people who do not abide by these, generally, heterosexual rules) may be targeted for mistreatment, which may include sexual harassment, abuse, rape, shunning from social activities, and even murder, depending on the level of tolerance of that society.

Gender role, on the other hand, is a social construct which refers to a defined set of behavioral and social norms (within a given culture) that are considered socially acceptable for each gender. In other words, in some societies women are expected to behave in certain ways and men are expected to behave in a different way. Gender roles not only refer to expected social behaviors, but extend to other issues such as clothing, thoughts, feelings, expectations, formation of relationships, and others.

Unfortunately, these social constructs of gender roles are based on a person's biological makeup or sex. In other words, mainstream society generates the appropriate gender roles based on the fact that a person who has a vagina is a woman; conversely, if a person has a penis, he is a man. When a person identifies himself a transgendered or third gender, complications arise within mainstream society. How is a transgendered person supposed to dress, think, and relate to others? Once again, depending on the level of tolerance of that society, the non-conformist may face different levels of mistreatment by other members of society which may include sexual harassment, abuse, shunning from social activities, and even murder.

That being said, there are words and terms in our vocabulary related to women that carry denigrating definitions, such as, spinster, cunt, whore, bitch, to name but a few. Once again, it is the third wave feminist belief that such words should be reclaimed back into mainstream language with a new meaning rather than simply censor the words altogether from our vocabularies. One of most frequently used words is bitch, which literally refers to the female of a dog. However, for many centuries the word has been used as a derogatory term to insult a woman or to describe her as malicious, mean, spiteful, and even to refer to her as overly sexual.

It was, however, during the second wave when feminists began to reclaim the word bitch. Joreen, in her *BITCH Manifesto*[24] clearly states that a bitch is a woman who is strong, capable, beautiful, efficient, and many other attributes all of which serve to take away the negative connotations of the word as employed in society to degrade women.

The trend of reclaiming this same word has continued throughout the years, and has continued to devalue its derogatory meanings. In her 1997 hit "Bitch," Meredith Brooks embraces the term by describing herself as a bitch as one the many attributes—lover, child, mother, sinner, etc.—that make up her persona.

Bitch Magazine is a response to such women's magazines as *Vogue, Self,* and others which present a conventional or pop culture view of women. *Bitch* offers its readers a different perspective (a feminist perspective) in its explorations of gender issues, sexuality, and power, among others, and includes interviews with people from all walks of life. *Bitch* also presents reviews of different topics which range from art to movies to books to television shows. Their mission is to "provide and encourage an empowered, feminist response to mainstream media and popular culture."[25] Because they have a diverse audience, they are able to explore and question topics as well as promote activism and social change. By calling itself "Bitch" the magazine clearly takes a stance. "When it's being used as an insult, 'bitch' is an epithet hurled at women who speak their minds, who have opinions and

24 *The BITCH Manifesto* by Joreen in http://www.uic.edu/orgs/cwluherstory/jofreeman/joreen/bitch.htm.
25 *Bitch Magazine*: About Us. in http://www.bitchmagazine.org/about

don't shy away from expressing them, and who don't sit by and smile uncomfortably if they're bothered or offended. If being an outspoken woman means being a bitch, we'll take that as a compliment."[26]

Body Image

Never has there been such stress on a woman's body image as in the last several decades, beginning with the Twiggy look back in the '60s through to today's size zero for models. Throughout history, beauty has changed its meaning, and we have come to a period in life where thin (sometimes dangerously so according to medical standards) is the desired standard of female beauty. A cross-cultural look at beauty will reveal that standards differ from country to country. For example, up until recently, facial hair was a sign of beauty in some Indian communities; a round face is much coveted in the Chinese culture, whereas in Hawaii and the Philippines large women are considered beautiful. In fact, in our culture, up until not long ago, as can be seen in nineteenth-century paintings, beautiful women were on average heavier set than what they are today. Even Marilyn Monroe, the sex symbol of the 1950s, would have been seen as overweight by today's standards.

By the end of the '80s and beginning of the '90s, there was a renewed and reviewed look at women. Silicone breasts were beginning to make waves, and women suddenly realized that the perfect breast was in vogue. At the same time, fashion was fast becoming heavily influenced by pornography, and designers like

26 Ibid.

Calvin Klein were eroticizing teenagers in most of its advertisements. In fact, many clothing designers began to use teenage girls that looked younger than their age to pose (in provocative poses) for children's clothing, giving the new children's (mainly girls') fashion the sex appeal of pop stars. The message, then and now, though in different forms, is still the same: the perfect woman. The sexual woman.

When *The Beauty Myth* by Naomi Wolf came out in 1991, it revolutionized the world (at least for women) and though it did have its share of backlash (in which the media several times accused Wolf of stating that it was wrong for women to shave their legs and wear lipstick and so forth) it was quite a sensation. The book gave many women hope and empowerment. For many women, the book represented a non-capitalistic and non-patriarchal view of beauty that conflicted with the narrow-minded establishment that had, since the last decade, reacted violently against feminism and the views of what woman should be. In fact, in the '80s, the word "feminism" had become a second f-word for many people, including then president Ronald Reagan, whose Republican government spanned almost the entire decade.

The Beauty Myth, then, gave many women a different look at their own lives. Now they looked at their own bodies and did not feel inadequate or ugly, but rather, they learned to appreciate that all women are different, and all human bodies are different. Age is not something that has to be fought against with anti-ageing creams or hair dyes . . . On the contrary, by learning to embrace white (salt-and-pepper) hair, many women have found new ways of expressing themselves and their individual beauty.

However, commercial industries and capitalism continue to place new criteria into effect not only in the Western world, but in other cultures as well, as in the case of India and some Latin American societies, where white skin is more desirable and encapsulates more desirable traits in the new concept of female beauty—a concept that is an extrapolation from Western cultures.

Another issue with the notion of female beauty is weight. Though being overweight has medical implications, so does being extremely thin. In their stride for perfection, models, actresses, and women who follow the popular trends sometimes develop eating disorders or, worse, are on the verge of becoming anorexic by medical standards, and this, too, is a question of social concern.

For many feminists, the issue of body weight is seen as a way of social control in more ways than one, and an issue that has generated the advertising industry millions of dollars annually. Because the prefect body is directly linked with the economy, a market has developed which survives on the inadequacies of the female body. Contradictory messages are given to women about their worth in terms of how beautiful (meaning thin) they look. At the same time, the undercurrent message is that beauty is somehow linked with sexual attractiveness, and by achieving these two attributes women will be automatically guaranteed success and happiness.

Spas, gyms, creams, lotions, diet programs, and a thousand other markets have sold, and continue to sell, their products to women who are constantly searching for that ultimate goal in life. This is not to say that men are exempt from the pressure of having to uphold or endorse the idea of the perfect man. While, indeed, men are subjected to their own pressures which dictate that the ideal man is wealthy and powerful, for men there is no standard that states that in order to be rich you have to look a certain way.

Wealth and power are in no way restricted by weight, height, standards of beauty, color, or age. However, in an attempt at trying to cash in on a hitherto poorly tapped market, the male standard of perfection has shifted its focus and now hones in on a man's physical strength: the classical six-pack, the well-defined torsos, and the bulging biceps and triceps are the image of today's man. Even if a man's body is a little on the chubby side and not as well sculpted as the epitome of the ideal man (as fashion and marketing would desire), man still maintains the role of protector while the woman's physique— emphasizing such disproportionate thinness— reinforces, more than ever, the notion that she is weak and needs protection from the man.

According to Ms. Wolf, body weight and beauty are employed in our society with a political intent. She states in *The Beauty Myth* that, "The stronger women were becoming politically, the heavier the ideals of beauty would bear down on them, mostly in order to distract their energy and undermine their progress."[27] In fact, if one analyses things carefully, for the first time in the history of humanity, women have had more money and power than ever before, women have had more legal, social, and political recognition

27 Wolf, Naomi. 2002. *The Beauty Myth: How Images of Beauty are Used Against Women.* Harper Perennial, p. 3

than ever before, however, on a physical level, women are nowhere near being emancipated at all.

When one analyzes the images of women in the media, we see that many of the pretty and thin women tend to be working outside of the home in jobs that, judging from their expensive clothes and jewelry, are well paid. These images of these ideal women are aimed at the general public and, as such, are generally of white middle- and upper-class women with an underrepresentation of African-American, Asian American, and any other minority group. It is only when advertisers target a particular group that one gets to see a representation of non-white women. The issue of race aside, there are other more subtle but equally concerning messages permeating images of women in advertisements. In other words, by the mere fact that thin women are successful, pretty, and happy, then the opposite must hold true—fat women are lazy, greedy, miserable, undesirable, and definitely, not beautiful.

Women who are overweight are discriminated upon, generally shunned in our society, and made to feel ashamed of being overweight because of the implication that their excess weight is caused by some physiological or psychological problem. Not all people understand that whereas being obese may pose risks to our health, so does the extreme thinness that women are bombarded with daily in every form and fashion, from advertisements (in magazines, newspapers, and the television) to mannequin displays and shops that do not carry anything above a size six because anything above that is already bordering on the overweight and therefore belonging in the large section.

At the same time that our society advertises how delicious junk food and fast foods are, women are bombarded with negative feelings of self-worth, social ridicule, hostility, and even job discrimination because they do not conform to the standard of thin. The end result of all this hype on weight is that there are as many diets as there are people endorsing them, and the idea of eating (for women) has become a national obsession in which a salad or a yogurt are seen as a woman's main choice of food—not for their healthy nutritional values, but because these foods are very low in calories.

According to the National Eating Disorders Association (NEDA), in the United States, approximately ten million females and one million males are currently struggling with eating disorders like anorexia and bulimia.[28]

Some disturbing statistics found in their research shows that in females aged between ten and thirty-nine, the incidence of bulimia tripled between the years 1988 and 1993. Because these disorders are difficult to recognize even by parents of younger girls, they pose an even worse threat to the well-being of the person because many times the people involved are afraid, do not recognize the symptoms, and, therefore, go untreated until it is too late. Both anorexia and bulimia are life-threatening disorders. Due to the high incidence of female targeting by the media to diet and strive for thinness, in 2005, the NEDA conducted a research among fifteen hundred adults (both male and female).

28 National Eating Disorders Association. In http://www. nationaleatingdisorders.org/information-resources/general-information. php

These are some of their results[29]:

- Over one-half of teenage girls and nearly one-third of teenage boys use unhealthy weight control behaviors such as skipping meals, fasting, smoking cigarettes, vomiting, and taking laxatives.
- 42% of 1st-3rd grade girls want to be thinner.
- 81% of 10 year-olds are afraid of being fat.
- The average American woman is 5'4' tall and weighs 140 pounds. The average American model is 5'11' tall and weighs 117 pounds.
- Most fashion models are thinner than 98% of American women.
- 46% of 9-11 year-olds are sometimes or very often on diets, and 82% of their families are sometimes or very often on diets.
- 91% of women recently surveyed on a college campus had attempted to control their weight through dieting, 22% dieted often or always.
- 25% of American men and 45% of American women are on a diet on any given day.
- Americans spend over $40 billion on dieting and diet-related products each year.

The NEDA also found the following facts about the media's influence in our daily lives, but especially so on women:

- The average U.S. resident is exposed to approximately 5,000 advertising messages a day.
- For adolescent girls, their main source of information about women's health issues comes from the media.

29 National Eating Disorders Association. Statistics: Eating Disorders and Their Precursors. In http://www.nationaleatingdisorders.org/uploads/file/Statistics Updated Feb 10, 2008 B.pdf

- Women's magazines have 10.5 times more advertisements and articles promoting weight loss than men's magazines do.
- Many teen magazines have articles about fitness or exercise plans; 74% of the magazines analyzed cited "to become more attractive" as a reason to start exercising, and 51% noted the need to lose weight or burn calories.
- The average young adolescent watches 3 to 4 hours of TV per day. A study of 4,294 network television commercials revealed that 1 out of every 3.8 commercials send some sort of attractiveness message, telling viewers what is or is not attractive.

For third wave feminists, the challenge is to bring back self-respect and empower women who face a losing battle against the commercialization of femaleness in our societies. Many self-awareness, self-help, and motivational groups are there to help women achieve self-love and improve their self-esteem through a host of different activities such as supporting magazines that promote women and their achievements and who have not been overly airbrushed to create a false image of women, writing letters to magazines and clothing stores explaining why the women they represent are false images of women, attending courses and lectures which deal with race and gender studies, forming chat groups and workshops which teach women about body weight and variations of weight throughout their lives. Some groups encourage women to feel comfortable with their weight first before gradually decreasing it, in stages, to more healthy standards.

Many of these groups help women understand health problems associated with eating disorders and, at the same time they teach women about the benefits of exercise and the importance of eating a healthy and balanced diet for their overall well-being. Though for many feminists widespread rebellion of what society dictates would be the most desirable answer to these social problems, such measures are idealistic and, instead, pamphlets, alternative magazines, and publications have made their way into mainstream society in an attempt at changing the cultural attitude and instilling, in society at large, a more tolerant view of body size and beauty in general.

Many women's groups focus on the negative "isms" (racism, sexism, ageism, etc) which are, according to many feminists, nothing more than social wedges driven in to create discord amongst women. By focusing on these topics, awareness groups strive to give their participants an alternative of who women are, with the desired outcome of changing women's attitudes about themselves and other women. By women changing their way of thinking and embracing the struggles of other women in a joint effort to succeed, the woman of today will learn to appreciate that other women are struggling beside her, and together they can levy a war against discrimination, prejudice, and ridicule. As we stand today, society continues to make a mockery of women by offering her a place in society (be it in politics or the business world), but at the same time taking the value of her performance away from her by focusing on her beauty and weight attributes rather than on her character and intelligence which got her there in the first place.

According to third wave feminists, the age-long focus on the female body which continues to handcuff and gag women has to be shifted if women are going to demand respect and equality from their male counterparts. Because of this, the third wave has brought a new slant into the thinking woman of today. By valuing diversity (in color, body shape and size, ethnic background, etc.) women hold the power to dismantle the biases and prejudices they confront in our society. By battling against the predominant injustices and inequalities, women are ensuring for themselves and for future generations the guarantee that new laws will be implemented—new laws, which, once and for all, value women for their true worth within society.

Other Areas

There are many other issues that have become part of the third wave feminist agenda. Much of the work was started during the second wave when it became an apparent issue that affected women adversely. Though race, sexuality, and social class are at the core of the third wave feminist fight, they also look at issues that center around the workplace, such as career advancement, sexual harassment, policies that affect single mothers and pregnant women on maternity leave, welfare, and child care.

Third wave feminists bring attention to unhealthy views of womanhood especially in the media which, in our society, have taken the form of eating disorders (anorexia and bulimia), portraying women as sexual objects, and depicting women as empty-headed glamour dolls interested only in their looks. Third wave feminists have responded in a variety of ways. One way, for example, is to have more of a positive female impact in pop culture.

Music has, for a long time, been dominated by men, especially punk. The Riot Grrrl (sometimes spelled Riot Grrl) movement began in the early 1990s and was a hybrid of alternative rock and punk as a response to the macho attitude inherent in punk. The misspelling of the word "girl" is a deliberate transformation to a growl, which in turn reclaims the word "girl" from the negative connotations given to it by our culture.

Because of their ideology, many of these bands did not have formal musical training. Women bands saw this not only as an outlet to express their artistic talents, but more importantly, as a resistance to abuse and harassment of women since Riot Grrrl lyrics often address issues of female empowerment, sexual abuse, rape, and domestic abuse among other topics. Riot Grrrl bands also place emphasis on female identity, taking a stance against large corporations which perpetuate the marginalized role of women. Instead, they stress the importance of self-sufficiency and self-reliance, and true to their word, these groups shunned the major record labels by signing with independent labels. Besides being a music scene, the Riot Grrrls also offer women zines in which to express their writings and in which to voice important political and social issues. Some of the most famous bands are Bikini Kill, Bratmobile, Jack Off Jill, Free Kitten, and many others.

In the world of rap a similar phenomenon has also taken place. Rap with its characteristic rhyming to the beat of background music is a genre employed as a mode of self-expression and social reflection especially by the African-American, who uses rap as a form of storytelling to expound the harsh realities of life. Until about fifteen years ago or so, female rappers were generally in the background as backup singers or dancers. But that soon changed as more and more women found themselves the object of sexual subjugation and degradation.

One of the most memorable names in rap music that came into the feminist limelight as well as into a court case, is 2 Live Crew. Not only was their album *As Nasty As They Wanna Be* graphically explicit in their specific sexual content, the songs were also humiliating, degrading, and violent against women. In their songs women are portrayed as cunts, hos, and they employed an infinite variety of definitions for the word bitch in which to portray women, such as raggedy bitches, sorry-ass bitches, lowdown slimy-ass bitches, and many others. In short, the songs did nothing more than engender sexual violence toward women.

Feminist rap came as a response, not just to this particular band, but as a response to rap as a genre in which women are a commodity and where girls who partake in sex automatically become whores; yet boys make use of sex to grow up to be men.

Feminist rap has its roots in women's blues which also uses lyrics to empower women and to dispute the macho role prominent in these songs. Just like women's blues, feminist rap focuses on demanding equal treatment for women, it promotes the importance of women, and above all, feminist rap lets men know that they can be dominant too. Among some of the most influential women in feminist rap are Queen Latifah (born Dana Elaine Owens), who began singing as Ladies Fresh, then went on to work with Flavor Unit. In her album *Black Reign* (1993)

Latifah confronts male sexual violence, debunking the myth that women are "hos"; Salt-N-Pepa, another influential name in female rap, makes use of sexual speech to downplay men by letting them know that women can be dominant too. In their songs, women are not submissive and definitely not inhibited in their sexual desires, therefore, they break the stereotype of women being the sexual toys of men. In fact their 1993 hit "Shoop" clearly shows the opposite since they show no inhibitions whatsoever in discussing their sexual desires and fantasies for men. Meanwhile, the video for the song portrays men playing objectified roles since the cameras deliberately change focus from the men's torsos to their buttocks, then panning to the women who clearly see them as objects of their sexual desire. The lyrics are powerful conveying the message that lust is acceptable and enjoyable without having to be demeaning or degrading to either party—a message which invariably suffuses male rap.

British born Monie Love (born Simone Wilson and protégé of Queen Latifah) is another influential name in women's rap, and she uses a deliberate choice of language to address the issue (stereotypical of male rap) that women need to be sexually submissive. Just like Queen Latifah, Monie Love raps about her intolerance for male aggression, oppression of women, violence both in the home and outside, and any form of subjugation, rejecting the men who put women in those positions. Monie Love, with her powerful lyrics, refuses to be placed in the stereotypical role of the African-American woman, and instead, by clever use of language, changes the image of women to more powerful, empowered, secure, and positive human beings.

As times continue to change, so have the attitudes that shape the woman of today. Today, there are many women who have made a name for themselves in the female rap scene, among them Eve, Sole, Charlie Baltimore, and Mia-X to name just a few.

Clashes and Criticisms

Not all has been plain sailing for the feminist movement throughout the years, especially now with the third wave. Indeed, there have always been many areas that have raised a number of issues within society and have made feminists the number one public enemy for as long as they have been around and continue to maintain the title of the other f-word.

Unfortunately for the movement, not all feminists agree with each other, and different factions have arisen—in some cases totally splitting off into their own groups—throughout the history of the women's movement. Conflicts, quarrels, agenda disagreements, and divergence have plagued the women's movement, not only from society at large, but from within the ranks. Three of the most heated debates/concerns among the feminists of today are the following:

Reproductive Rights

From as far back as the second wave, the abortion debate has polarized feminists into those who are pro-life and those who are pro-choice.

For pro-choice feminists, the debate over abortion is one that focuses on the status of women within her society. That a woman has the right to choose to be pregnant or not means that she can sidestep or avoid patriarchal values which force women into certain roles (that of mother or housewife). Though the roles of mother and housewife are not inherently demeaning, in some cultures these roles serve to relegate women to a status that demeans her.

While many feminists are both mother and housewife, it has been their choice, and to have this choice implies that when a woman places herself in those roles it is with the knowledge and understanding that she is not second class to men. By fighting for a woman's right to choose, feminism is fighting for a woman's inalienable rights, a woman's innate worth, and, at the same time, fighting for every woman's right to be treated as a respected and respectable, valuable, and talented member of society not merely as a baby-making and looking-after-husband-and-children human being.

The main reason why feminism sees the role of mothers as second-class citizens is because women leave their talents and careers aside to concentrate solely on their husbands' and children's careers and lives. Many a time women are left either widowed or divorced at an age that is very difficult for them to have access to health care, education, and employment since their lives have been dedicated to others but herself. These situations place undue stress on women, and many struggle to make ends meet and often lead miserable lives. Feminism sees this as a loss of a perfectly valuable member of society being pushed to the background for no other reason than to comply with impractical patriarchal values.

Pro-life feminists on the other hand, though they do not disagree with women becoming equal to men, see the issue of abortion differently. For them, abortion is another tactic employed by the patriarchal culture to keep women in submission. This is done by the simple method of not encompassing motherhood in the overall structure of society.

These groups of feminists argue that the beginning of discrimination arises with the realization that women and men are different anatomically. Women, because of their lack of a penis, do not succeed in life and are relegated to second class, and her only way to come out of that lower status is to become pregnant so that she can adapt to the demands placed upon her by the patriarchal culture. Socially, women's beauty is defined by how thin she is. A pregnant woman is not considered pretty by the social standards of society, and by terminating a pregnancy, women are succumbing to the social pressure to be thin and therefore beautiful. In short, women are living their lives according to a set of standards created by men in their definition of womanhood.

Pro-life feminists also posit that when women are pregnant they feel beautiful and in charge of their bodies and their lives. However, social standards in our culture have been created in which a pregnancy has become a medical condition, precarious sometimes, and which must be controlled and monitored to ensure its term comes to a natural and healthy end. By not embracing a pregnancy, a woman is not embracing her body nor is she embracing her life, but rather she is defining herself according to the standards of a male-dominated society.

Through the legalization of abortions, then, the patriarchal culture is allowed to continue to manage pregnancies while, at the same time, keeping women as second-class citizens. This is done by alienating women from identifying with their own bodies and with their own feelings of self-worth. Worse, instead of liberating women, the right to have a legal abortion has now made women less equal to a man.

By choosing to have an abortion, a woman is conforming to male rules and accepting the fact that, in our society, there are no provisions made for pregnant women or for women with small children, and therefore, to be politically, economically, and socially active, a woman must not have children. Hence, rather than fight for a society to be more embracing of pregnancies and children while allowing women to be active in all spheres of life, pro-choice feminism continues to allocate the role of caretakers of children to women, and by implication, keep men away from any responsibility pertaining to children.

According to Germaine Greer, "What women 'won' was the 'right' to undergo invasive procedures in order to terminate unwanted pregnancies, unwanted not just by them, but by their parents, their sexual partners, the governments who would not support mothers, the employers who would not employ mothers, the landlords who would not accept tenants with children, the schools that would not accept students with children."[30]

Because the issue of abortion is fraught with disagreement, misconceptions have arisen from anti-feminist factions (mainly anti-abortionists) who accuse feminism of their ultimate goal to control fertility. This is far from the truth. According to feminism, and especially third wave, the goal is to

30 Germaine Germaine. 1999. *The Whole Woman*. Alfred A. Knopf. p. 92.

make women free to control their bodies because society at large has no right to control a woman's body; by doing so, women are more equal with men. Aside from that, there is the added patriarchal insult to (and subjugation of) a woman that by denying her the right to an abortion, a woman has less rights than a fetus. From the pro-choice feminist point of view, this implies that a breathing, conscious, and living member of society is seen as a lesser form of human being than a fetus which has not yet been born, and which is without thoughts and unconscious. Therefore, denying women their right to a legal abortion diminishes women in society.

Up until abortion became legal, if a woman became pregnant, she only had two recourses at her disposal: a) continue with an unwanted pregnancy, or b) to undergo an illegal (and unsafe) abortion that more often than not put her life at risk.

Though significant progress has been made in the area, a host of new issues have arisen that still pose controversial arguments both from feminists and from society at large. For example:

- The mommy track – should women continue to compete with men for advancement in their careers while balancing a family on the other hand? Should there be a law making businesses accommodate women's family duties and responsibilities? Or should there be a law making men a more integral part of his family?
- Surrogate mothers – does this also fall under the label of "a woman's freedom to control her body"? Will rent-a-womb become a business reality in the future? What are the social, economic, and ethical implications of such a business?

- Pornography (in printed material and music) – is pornography and extreme sexual content and degradation of women freedom of speech? Are women who engage in pornography exercising their right and freedom to control their bodies?

Lack of Single Cause for Third Wave Feminism

Though at first glance it may not seem to be such a big issue for many women within the movement, for others it is of great importance since it seems as if the third wave is the catch-all with no agenda in particular, but with plans and programs for everything. The main criticism is that the first wave fought for and attained the right to vote for women and the second wave pushed women forward into the workforce, ending sex discrimination, and giving women equal rights. In contrast, the third wave seems to lack a plan of action, and for some critics, as stated elsewhere, it is not a wave per se, but an extension of the previous one. What is the most outstanding feature of third wave feminism is the young feminist culture that seems to permeate all groups that identify themselves as feminist.

The third wave feminist is one that has grown up in a feminist world created by the previous generation of feminists, and as such, much of the influence in the third wave comes from the older generation of women. Second wave feminism is intertwined with a political agenda that touched the very core of a society in turmoil, be it because of the Vietnam War, the Civil Rights Movement, or the simple fact that women wanted their voices heard. In short, it was a collectivist mentality that pushed women forward in a male-dominated world.

Third wave feminists, on the other hand, are more individualistic in their outlook and approach, and they have been brought up in, and influenced by, a world of consumerism, the emergence of the Internet, computer technology, zines, hip-hop, and other factors that were not present in the '60s, '70s, and even '80s. This is not to say that third wave feminism is selfish, lost in their ideas, or next to useless. Not at all. Each generation has their way of addressing social issues and women issues with the most convenient method of the times, and whereas the preferred method of the second wave feminist were discourses and dialogues, the present times are made up of blogs and e-zines.

This badly defined line separating these two groups of feminists is a phenomenon present today that did not exist between the first and second waves simply because the time period separating them was far greater than that separating the second and third waves. Indeed, because the feminists of today are so diverse and belong to two generations of feminism, the feminists of today pose themselves pertinent questions depending on whether they belong to the older generation or the new one. For veteran feminists, the question is whether the young women of today (in their twenties and thirties) actually appreciate what was done thirty years ago. At the same time, the younger women question whether women in their fifties and sixties understand the problems of young women today.

The rift between us and them is a theme that has emerged several times between the two generations of feminists. The political and social climate of yore has turned less revolutionary and more reactionary, bringing with it an emphasis on a more me/I oriented culture than before. In this new culture, the woman of today has left family values aside and become more career oriented. At the same time, a backlash has occurred fueled by media stories of career women of the '80s who regret not having had children. This has led to a new set of values which the women of today have assimilated. In taking advantage of the successes of feminism, the new woman of today totally ignores the urgency to continue to fight for the rights of women, a reticence that has contributed to pushing feminism to the side, and in many cases, once again, young feminists have unwittingly dishonored the cause.

In countering the older feminists' criticisms concerning a lack of a single plan of action, third wave feminists present the logic of their actions by suggesting that more agendas means more freedoms. Their rationale is that by focusing on different issues affecting the lives of women (not just abortion, economic parity, and equality in the workplace—the central topics of the second wave), women are given the power to simultaneously address and remedy a host of other issues that still plague society and which continue to diminish the value of women in their culture. In fact, this broad outlook does not automatically mean a dissipation of the new wave of feminist, as older feminists suggest, but rather, it suggests a greater freedom of action. From music to arts in general to prison reform, the third wave continues to offer their own unique perspective and offers a new space for women to express themselves in their own unique ways.

The question for many remains: who are the third wave feminists? Are they grassroots activists or are they women with a lot of attitude and nothing to lose?

The Fear of Post-feminism

For many scholars who do not believe in the various waves of feminism, the notion of an end to feminism or a post-feminism era sometime in the future may seem inevitable. It is an interesting thought since the term may imply an era in which society no longer needs the watchful eye of feminists to maintain the lawful rights of women. Such a notion would imply a complete and utter equality between the genders which some deem as utopian. However, this issue arises not from anything other than the fact that feminism is no longer as much in the limelight as it was during the '60s, '70s, and '80s—three decades of high social tension during which many battles were won by women and for women.

Recent speculation and analysis of the third wave of feminists has resulted in the idea that feminism will not be able to sustain itself in the future. Indeed, several organizations, including the New York City Young Women's Network, have ceased to exist due to funding problems and, more alarming, not able to reach out to those for whose benefit it was created. Many young women today do not consider themselves feminists because the word carries a host of implications that they, perhaps, do not identify with. Many women, though they fight for reproductive freedom or against parental consent laws, do not see this as activism or as a way of empowering themselves, least of all, they do not see it as a political necessity.

Being a feminist today means that the young woman of today has to shed the definition of the feminist of yore and has to accept her present rights, not as given rights, but as fought for rights. This trend is very much present in our societies today, and even though young women all over the world are still being sexually harassed, raped, deprived of an education, and denied social status, they do not always recognize the value of challenging and fighting against a common perpetrator.

For the older feminist, a way to ensure that feminism does not die out into history is to effectively analyze goals and pull together strengths and skills in order to continue addressing those goals. By challenging the usual fears of color or race or differences between and among women, feminism stands a chance of its continuation into the future.

Be that as it may, for others, the idea of post-feminism is ludicrous as women are nowhere near being equal to men in any way. This means that women will continue to wage a war against the establishment until, little by little, the gap separating gender and inequality lessens into nothingness.

For the young generation of women carrying the torch of feminism, concepts that are generally swept under the carpet will pose as the next generation of challenges to overcome. Until sexual harassment, sexual discrimination, domestic violence, and host of other new topics are a thing of the past, the next generation of feminists will continue to fight using whatever means they have at their disposal, from consciousness-raising groups to guerilla theatre. If history has taught humanity anything at all it is that at every turn of the way there will be a group of women waiting to fight inequality in their own form or fashion. It is the revolution of the mind that counts when it comes to forever changing a social malaise.

IMPACTS OF FEMINISM ON SOCIETY

One way or another, feminism has affected every single imaginable aspect of society. Due to the vastness of this topic, it would be beyond the scope of this book to try to touch upon every single area that has felt the impacts of feminism. Instead, only a few areas will be briefly touched upon to show how far and wide feminism has made its mark.

Gender-neutral Language

The issue of whether language was inclusive of both genders or not was not of much concern until the 1970s and 1980s when feminists realized that language (especially the English language) was male inclusive and female exclusive. Though many other languages in the world, for example, romance languages (French, Spanish, Italian, Portuguese and so forth) clearly are gendered (male and female nouns, pronouns, adjectives, etc.), English is not so gendered-defined along grammatical lines, however, many nouns show a bias toward the male gender.

Whether this reflects a male dominance or superiority remains the major point of contention between those who believe that language should be neutral and those who do not. Aside from this issue, historically speaking, in some cases, words and expressions have been lost and are not used anymore. In other cases, they have changed their meaning from what they used to be at one time or another. This is seen very clearly in nouns. Many of the nouns that have changed their meaning through the ages, for whatever reason, are words that refer to women. One interesting example is the word "mistress." According to the Merriam-Webster Online, the word "mistress" comes from the Middle English *maistresse*, and from the Anglo-French *mestresse*, which is the feminine form of *mestre* or master. Once upon a time, several centuries ago, it denoted "a woman who has power, authority, or ownership: as (a:) the female head of a household (b:) a woman who employs or supervises servants (c:) a woman who is in charge of a school or other establishment d: a woman of the Scottish nobility having a status comparable to that of a master."[31]

Somehow, through the years, the word "mistress" has evolved into its present connotations, and today, it denotes a man's kept woman, or a man's lover. In other words, gone are the power, authority, and status that the word once carried with it. Interestingly enough, though the word "master" has also gone through its share of evolution through the years, the changes have not been as dramatic. Once again, according to the Merriam-Webster's Online Dictionary, "master" comes from the Old English *magister* and Anglo-French *meistre*, and both come from Latin *magister*. Even as far back as the twelfth century, "master" meant "(1a:) (1): a male teacher (2): (a:) person holding an academic degree higher than a bachelor's but lower than a doctor's (b:) *often capitalized*: a revered religious leader (c:) a worker

---

31 *Merriam-Webster's Online Dictionary*, in http://www.merriam-webster.com/dictionary/mistress

or artisan qualified to teach apprentices (d:) (1): an artist, performer, or player of consummate skill (2): a great figure of the past (as in science or art) whose work serves as a model or ideal (2a:) one having authority over another : RULER, GOVERNOR (b:) one that conquers or masters : VICTOR, SUPERIOR <in the new challenger the champion found his master> (c:) a person licensed to command a merchant ship (d:) (1): one having control (2): an owner especially of a slave or animal e: the employer especially of a servant (f:) (1) *dialect*: HUSBAND (2): the male head of a household (3a:) (1) *archaic* : MR. (2): (a) youth or boy too young to be called *mister*—used as a title (b:) the eldest son of a Scottish viscount or baron (4a:) (a:) presiding officer in an institution or society (as a college) (b:) any of several officers of court appointed to assist (as by hearing and reporting) a judge."[32]

Though its usage for "a youth or boy too young to be called mister" may have been dropped out of current usage, as can be noted, contrary to the female counterpart, the word "master" still remains a title of honor and retains the implicit power, status, and authority that has gone along with it for the past nine hundred years.

On another vein, a promiscuous man is a player, but a promiscuous woman is a slut or a whore, where once again, language has managed to give the male word a less negative implication or overtone than that given to the female noun.

Once upon a time, spinster and bachelor meant roughly the same thing, that is, a person (one a female

---

32 *Merriam-Webster's Online Dictionary*, in http://www.merriam-webster.com/dictionary/master

and one a male, respectively) that was not married. Today, a bachelor carries the undertone of an ageless happy-go-lucky man who lives life to his fullest and who is not yet willing to commit to the seriousness of settling down and marrying a woman. A spinster, on the other hand, is an unmarried, older woman past her prime of youth. The word carries the implication of a lonely, perhaps strict or uptight woman who lacked the charm to enchant a man into blissful marriage.

Another set of words that until recently denoted male superiority or denoted inequality in society are those words of power and authority. Historically, there is a perfectly reasonable explanation for this and that is women, until not long ago, did not have the right to vote much less hold such positions of power. The only way in which a woman could hold a position of power was if she were born into a titled position, as in the case of a queen. Thanks to the women's movement, women are now capable of holding high-ranking posts in society, and because they are doing so more and more as time goes by, such words as governor, mayor, chairman, etc., have had to be modified in the last few decades to encompass a female counterpart.

The same holds true for professions and careers (policeman, fireman, postman, or mailman), which have also undergone a change to encompass many female members that now are part of those groups. Other professions have undergone slight changes in duties through the years as they have changed from male to female or vice versa.

One such case is that of the secretary. Historically, a secretary (better known today as clerk or admin) used to be a man who trained to become assistant or aide to professionals or men who worked in commerce. In fact, when Sir Isaac Pitman founded his school for teaching the system of shorthand he developed, the first students that enrolled were all men. As the years went by and the first typewriter was invented, more women entered the field. It is said that because women's fingers are smaller and thinner they are more adept at fine motor coordination, and so they became more expert in the area and made better stenographers in general. With the advent of the First World War, women flooded the market, and before long, women were dominating the posts of secretaries.

As time elapsed, the responsibilities of a secretary changed and modified to what they are at present. For example, a male secretary of one hundred years ago was a man who carried out a different set of tasks than merely dictation taking and typing as is the stereotypical case of many secretaries in the '60s and '70s. Once again, because women have never been seen as intelligent or worthy of any position of power or authority, bosses are, by definition, male, and the people who carry out the menial tasks of an office are the female secretaries employed for that very same reason.

In fact, after the Second World War, women who became widowed (and whose pensions were inadequate to survive on), or who were divorced, or who did not wish to go back to homemaking sought employment in many areas, one of those being as secretaries. Once again, with the help of government propaganda promoting the qualities of good women/wives, working women (secretaries) saw it as their duty to see to the overall comfort of her boss, from making his tea/coffee in the morning, to making sure that his well-being was cared for at all costs. In short, the female secretary's job was to make sure that her boss was just as well looked after in his office as he was at home. A good secretary was just as good as a wife.

Another area of much heated debate and of grave concern for feminists, which began with the second wave and has continued to the present day, is the word "man." The word "man," historically, has been used to talk about both sexes in an inclusive manner. One could argue that the reason for this is that men have always been the ones at the helm in terms of making and changing laws, and it has always been men who have gathered in committees, meetings, conferences, and assemblies to carry out such tasks. Since, by definition, women were not allowed in these decision-making activities, there was no need to address women since no women were present. Thus, documents were written with the implicitness that the word "man" automatically included women—after all, women were the property of men.

The words "human" and "woman" leave a lot to be desired and one cannot help but agree with staunch feminists that the word "woman" should be changed to something else that does not have the implication of "man" or an extension of one. In order to achieve that, feminists have often made use of variations of the word such as "wymming" or "wombyn" or "womyn" keeping the original pronunciation, but changing the spelling in an attempt at making the word completely unrelated to man and therefore rightful in its own terms.

By doing this, women shed connotations associated with the word—many of which have been used throughout the centuries to oppress and discriminate. At the same time, by reclaiming the word, a woman is redefining herself, spiritually, physically, and socially as an individual separate from men. Women are not a sub-category of man or an inferior variety of the human species and, as such, she demands to be acknowledged as a separate entity, whole and individual.

In other spheres of the English language, such as in the grammatical usage of pronouns, gender plays an important role. Once again, feminists have tried to propose a gender-neutral construct where women are not mere phantoms of speech. Such cases as the generic "he" (when referring to both male and female) make women disappear from speech and, therefore, women become the target of discrimination and exclusion from areas (for example, professions and schools) that make use of the distinction to, deliberately, maintain male exclusivity.

The most notable all-male college that began admitting women only after a lawsuit from the Department of Justice in 1990 is the Virginia Military Institute (VMI). In the lawsuit, the U.S. Department of Justice sued the school for discrimination, arguing that the school could not prevent women from joining based on gender.

In order to be more inclusive of both genders, proposed alternatives to the generic "he" are such constructs as "he or she," "she or he" and even "s/he." In many cases "they" is the proposed singular for dealing with the matter. Although there have been a lot of misinterpretations and objections, many regulating bodies have adopted the terms, and in the case of the Chicago Manual of Style, they have made "they," "them," and "their" grammatically acceptable as gender-neutral singular pronouns in English. Others have followed suit.

At the same time that women seek to be accepted as individuals separate from men, another issue women have to contend with is their invisibility when it comes to names and honorifics. Historically speaking, upon marriage women became automatically invisible. Women have always been the daughter of a man, and the wife of a man. Even the ritual practice of a wedding today continues to perpetuate the giving away of the daughter by her father to the new male proprietor of her life—her husband. Through this and the adamant practice of continuing a family lineage through the male, men's names are indelible in history, while women's are lost forever in time.

But it can have its drawbacks. One classic example is that of William Shakespeare. His name has totally disappeared from history by the simple fact that he and his wife only engendered female descendants. Although through oral history today someone could easily claim that they were the great-great-grandchild of that famous poet/writer, there are no physical historical records that would verify the claim, and so the lineage has disappeared along with the name.

This issue of invisibility has been plaguing the feminist cause for longer than may appear at first glance. In fact, as far back as the mid-nineteenth century, the practice of using the husband's first and last names to address a woman (for example, Mrs. Henry B. Stanton) was questioned by such women as Lucretia Mott and Elizabeth Cady Stanton among others.

The women's movement at that time was adamant that women should be addressed using their own first names, and though they accepted the use of their married names, some like Elizabeth Cady Stanton, kept her maiden name (Cady). Needless to say, these women vehemently opposed the idea of coverture, that is the notion proposed by William Blackstone in 1765 that stated, "By marriage, the husband and wife are one person in law: that is, the very being or legal existence of the woman is suspended during the marriage, or at least is incorporated and consolidated into that of the husband; under whose wing, protection, and *cover*, she performs everything; and is therefore called in our law-French a *feme-covert*, *foemina viro co-operta*; is said to be *covert-baron*, or under the protection and influence of her husband, her *baron*, or lord; and her condition during her marriage is called her *coverture*."[33]

It was for the very same reason of avoiding invisibility, as stated in another chapter, that the term "Ms" was created. Because women have historically been the property of men, there was never the need to use a title that gave women their own identity—they were either Miss (meaning daughter of a man) or Mrs. (wife of a man). At the same time, either title signifies to the outside world whether a woman is sexually available or not, and certainly whether she is eligible for marriage or not. The introduction of Ms as the equivalent of Mr. puts women on the same equal footing, that is, there is no overt indication of marital status.

Though many people may find gender-neutral language ridiculous and even offensive, it has been well researched, and conclusions have shown,

33 William Blackstone. (1979) *Commentaries on the Laws of England: A Facsimile of the First Edition of 1765-1769*, Vol. 1 University Of Chicago Press, pages 442-445.

without a doubt, that language shapes people's ways of thinking and, consequently, language has shaped human behaviors. Because language is a powerful tool that can easily influence and discriminate, care has to be taken with its usage, as it is this constant abuse of language that has reinforced many of the present behaviors that are in need of change in our society—especially those that discriminate. This can be clearly noted, for example, in the prevalent use of powerful words with an implied superiority which have historically been used to describe men. At the same time, words that express a sentiment of inferiority have always been used to describe women, i.e. the weaker sex.

Academic Disciplines

As second wave feminism grew in influence, so did student and faculty realize that something vital was being left out from mainstream academic studies. Modeled after such disciplines as African-American and Chicano studies, women's studies (sometimes also known as feminist studies) suddenly became an important discipline that would allow for the dissemination of women's plights within the history of humanity.

Women's studies is an interdisciplinary academic field that uses history, anthropology, sociology, and other disciplines to critique and explore societal norms, such as, class, gender, race, sexuality, and others, from a woman's perspective. It was established in 1970 as an experimental series of classes, and it became so popular that it grew to other schools and finally became accepted into the general curriculum of major universities. At the core of the curriculum, women's studies encouraged students to discuss and reflect upon social norms and values as they are in our societies today.

Today, women's studies is offered from an undergraduate level to a post-doctorate level, and it has widened its curricula to encompass a wide variety of topics, such as gender studies, queer and critical theories, among others. At the core of all these theories and studies is the idea that sexuality, sex, and gender are social constructs.

Though women's studies is not totally restricted to women's issues, it does try to dismantle the global oppression of women. Through the use of a host of disciplines such as poetry, literature, visual, and other forms of art, politics, economics, and other academic fields, women's studies researches, analyzes, and understands the factors that oppress women in different societies around the world; in doing so, it exposes to all members of those particular societies cultural inequalities and disparities with the hope that all members of society become participants in giving women a chance to create a space for themselves with the intended result of influencing all aspects of society.

Queer studies are another subject area that has become popular in the last few decades. Queer studies focuses on issues relating to gender identity and sexual orientation, focusing mainly on lesbian, gay, bisexual, transgender, and intersex people (LGBTI). In other words, queer studies examines the identity, lives, and history of queer people and issues raised by other academic fields of study such as biology, sociology, history, psychology, to name a few. The main question posed by this field of study is not simply what causes homosexuality, but rather, why sexuality should be such a central focus in some people's perspectives. Among some of the most prominent founding scholars are Michel Foucault, Judith Butler, Audre Lorde, and Eve Sedgwick.

Though still very much on the fringes in many countries, queer studies is slowly picking up followers as more and more countries become tolerant of homosexuality and more evidence is uncovered of gays and lesbians in history, challenging, at the same time, social constructs of sexuality and sexual identity.

Sexual Relationships and the Family

The whole nature of heterosexuality and heterosexual relationships has been questioned from the point of view of traditional morality, especially in recent years since homosexuals have become more active in their campaigning. With the increase in sexual openness and acceptance, the homosexual movement has increased in numbers while, at the same time, growing in the public eye. The lesbian, gay, bisexual, and transgender movement (LGBT) is now part of mainstream society and legally recognized in a vast number of countries around the world continuously demanding the same rights that heterosexual couples enjoy. In fact, the LGBT aims to promote visibility of different types of sexual orientation that go beyond what is considered the norm, that is, heterosexuality.

In all countries around the world, there is a standard or social construct of what the stereotype for female and male should be. These standards may differ from country to country, but what does not differ is that there is a traditional role for the male and a traditional role for the female that are different from each other. Generally speaking, males have always been dominant in Western societies, and females have been submissive. There are also biological differences between males and females. So, following general logic to make an argument for the worldwide accepted standard of heterosexuality as the only "norm," it makes sense that socially and biologically, males and females should be together for the purposes of procreation—though not necessarily for establishing a family.

These are the standards that have been eroded in the last several decades since the LGBT movement became openly visible. The fact that male/female differences in our society are becoming less rigid as time goes by plays an important role in the assimilation of other forms of gender identities, which, at the same time, break down other standards, such as the concept of the traditional marriage. Humans, by virtue of their capacity for reasoning and logic, are not bound by instincts that bind animals into particular behaviors, such as the sexual instinct. This has to be said with extreme caution since, in the past few years, the topic of sexuality has shed a lot of its prudishness as more researchers, unashamedly, delve into the private lives of animals. Animal research has shed very interesting results which leave no doubt that, for example, some animals (not just primates), both male and female, repeatedly engage in and enjoy sexual activities with members of their own gender—what could be called homosexual activity.

Though the argument may sound as if humans have the capacity to choose to act upon homosexual or heterosexual behaviors, the answer is not that simple. What makes a person desire someone of their own gender is not a choice. What is a choice is whether that true desire is repressed in order to comply with a social standard within a punitive society or not.

For many years, homosexuality has been repressed in a world which does not accept a union between two people of the same sex. Whatever the argument for that may be, the LGBT movement has slowly begun to change the social norm into a more accepting one by demanding from society an acceptance of a lifestyle that is compatible with who they are. The idea of compulsory heterosexuality is slowly eroding as the idea of same-sex partners moves in to take a legal place in some societies.

As more and more same-sex partners openly get married and openly demand the same rights that heterosexual couples enjoy, a new family concept has emerged. At the same time, the former biological argument for males to mate with females for the sole purpose of procreation has found a new way of bypassing sexual contact between the participants involved when making their new families. For female couples, sperm banks provide an alternative for acquiring the required essentials (i.e. the sperm); while for male couples, adoption is one of the preferred forms of starting a family.

As homosexuality becomes more widely accepted in our society, so are other forms of sexual identity becoming more recognized, and if not totally accepted—yet—they will be as tolerance to other forms of sexual identity continues to grow.

Relationships Between Men and Women

The traditional values and behaviours affecting men and women have undergone a complete overhaul. For as far back as history goes, males have always been the traditional breadwinners and women have been the sole keepers of home and family, a relationship that has maintained women dependent on men and, therefore, in a subordinate position. This situation has gradually changed, and the first step was made when women demanded the right to vote nearly a hundred years ago. Since then, both men and women have had to adapt to the new circumstances in which women no longer are seen as traditional homemakers while men go out and earn a wage to support the family. Rather, many women are choosing to postpone a family in order to educate themselves and to go out into the workforce to earn a wage. Indeed, the economic situation of many countries has demanded that women go out to earn a second salary to maintain the home as it is financially impossible to live on the salary of one spouse. Nevertheless, cost of living notwithstanding, many women today wish to be financially independent of their husbands/male partners, as well as having a life (meeting new people, making friends, expanding and broadening their knowledge) outside of the home.

The most important factor influencing women to seek out the workforce has been the women's movement. This has created new rights for women, which they now enjoy, thus creating a change in the power relationship between women and men.

These endeavours have not been without their share of conflict and backlash. Indeed, the new situation created by this shift in the relationship between men and women is the superwoman of today; a woman who now sees herself tending to the demands of a double shift: one outside the home and a second at home as she continues to carry out her traditional tasks of home keeping and child rearing. Unfortunately, this concept of the superwoman of today who is a successful businesswoman but continues to be a successful and dutiful wife/mother at home has created a lot of aggravation and stress to many women who struggle to raise a family by themselves and still maintain the feminine (mother/wife) identity imposed upon her by society—an image falsely created and hyped up by the media.

As women become more and more successful in their careers, so is there higher media attention to women who have dropped out of the "male rat race" to focus on home and family and give their children a better chance at education. Working women are often the ones to be quickly blamed when children do not do well in school. At the same time, it is important for fathers to be role models for their children, and society makes a big show of portraying the father at the center of the family. But it is a well-known fact that fathers rarely get called out of work when a child has any kind of problem in school. This is still the mother's responsibility.

For years, men have taken time to pursue their studies and careers, leaving wife and children temporarily so they can better themselves in order to give their families better financial support. Paradoxically, this does not seem to apply to women—

not even when a woman is a single mother raising a child on her own. Women who delay having children for the purposes of career advancement are seen, by some, as rather insensitive and uncaring since, in our society, it is the unequivocal desire of every woman to want to birth children.

Regardless of these issues, many women do succeed at handling both aspects of their lives and have continued to strive forward, demanding from a society of double-standards for childcare facilities in their workplaces, certain motherhood benefits, job and wage protection, flexible hours, as well as demanding from their male partners that they recognize their roles and responsibilities in family issues.

Religion

Once upon a time, the idea of women being ordained in any religion was as remote an idea as the notion that one day women would have the right to vote. Both notions have now become a reality. Today, women hold a place within various religious denominations as feminism has slowly, but surely, pushed its way to make these all-male institutions more accepting of women. In the more liberal branches of the Protestant faith, women have become clergy, and in Judaism, women have graduated from rabbinical schools and have been ordained as rabbis.

Conservative, Reform, Reconstructionist, and even Orthodox seminaries have gradually incorporated women, though the arguments against have been long and arduous. The Reform and Reconstructionist movements have been slightly more tolerant, the former talking about the ordination of women from as far back as 1922, and the latter actually ordaining a handful of women since 1968. For the Orthodox, on the other hand, the idea of women performing the duties of rabbi is still rather ludicrous. They will not accept female ordination by upholding and maintaining the age-long belief that women cannot receive *smicha.* In other words, women cannot be ordained because the act originated with Moses and has been passed down only to men.

With the help of very few male advocates, women continue with their plight by arguing that keeping women out of the religious sphere is a detriment to the faith. Women argue that they are an added asset to the interpretation of the great book by expanding definitions and re-evaluating traditional definitions concerning family and sexuality that have gone unquestioned. They also argue that women should be recognized for their intellectual accomplishments and spiritual attainments—both of which talents have been wasted so far—and because women would encourage the study of the Torah in the home.

Although the process is slow, progress into the ordination of women rabbis is increasing as the years go by, along with tolerance for such changes.

Generally speaking, throughout history, women have had to keep silent in matters of religion, but with feminism making women more visible in every sphere of life, this traditionally male-dominated area has succumbed to the recognition of women. With the exception of a handful of denominations such as Islam (where women imams are fighting to lead mixed-gender congregations in prayer), Mormons (the Church of Jesus Christ of Latter-day Saints), and

Roman Catholicism, every other denomination allows women to hold positions in which they can officiate. Today, there are female priests, clergy, deacons, and bishops within the Christian faith, as well as *purohits* and *pujaris* in Hinduism, rabbis (Judaism), *Bhikkhunis* or fully ordained Buddhist nuns, Shinto priest (Shinto), and *Fangzhang* or principal abbot (Taoism).

Feminism has also opened the doors to other forms of religion that had always been disreputable and discredited as blasphemous in the face of mainstream religions. Most of these neopagan religions emphasize the Goddess figure and female spirituality as being as important as that of the male counterpart, and they also place great emphasis on the importance of Nature and the environment as a whole, among other things. These religions are growing rapidly, especially among the younger generation who reject the patriarchal, sexist, and homophobic attitudes of traditional religions. One such example is that of the Wicca religion.

Women and Technology

Historically, women have been left out of much of what constitutes the fields of science and technology for the simple fact that these fields have always been the domains of men. As far as the Western world goes, religion and politics have created cultural stereotypes for both men and women, which have resulted in limiting women in their opportunities to a full education and, by implication, restricting women from developing their skills and abilities to their fullest potential.

Today, thanks to feminism, the number of women entering the fields of science and technology has incremented considerably and numbers have tripled and quadrupled in some fields. For example, in 2003, in the United States, 21 percent of the doctoral students in computing were women; and in the European Union, the number reached to almost 20 percent. In fact, in the United States alone, women now make more than 15 percent of the total number of engineers.

However, numbers do not seem to rise past a certain limit, and many scholars and researchers argue that this may be due to the fact that women continue to juggle home and work in their struggle to live up to the cultural stereotypes of female behavior within our social settings. Aside from that, schools continue to encourage women to participate in humanities-related fields rather than on hard-core science, such as, mathematics, physics, and chemistry.

In reality, women have always been a part of science, invention, and innovation. Through recorded history, women have been made invisible, and it is only now, in the last one hundred years, that women have made their voices public. Male-dominated societies have always denied women's intelligence, labeling them, instead, as intuitive. Given this label, it only stands to reason that their capacity for invention is heightened, since discovery and invention rely heavily on intuition. Indeed, many women have been the inventors of many a machine, but caught in the stereotypes of patriarchal societies where they had no voice or vote, so to speak, women had no option but to turn to a male (brother, father, husband, etc.) to have their invention patented.

One look at history shows that women were in charge of food gathering, cooking, and tending home. Once again, though there is no documentation for or against, those chores were a female domain, and it is reasonable to assume that many of the processes and inventions that deal with these areas should be attributed to women. Indeed, American women in the nineteenth century, struggling against prejudice, ridicule, and indifference, managed to patent a host of food processing items such as apple peelers, the hand-crank ice-cream freezer, steam cookers, ovens, vacuum processes for canning and for drying foods, and other cooking-related devices. All this without proper educational training in the field, or access to laboratories or workshops, and little or no funding to help them and, in some cases, not even the moral support of their own families.

In other traditionally female areas such as home and health, women have been the inventors of such diverse items such as the clothes wringer, anti-itch ointments, plus a host of natural remedies that range from the treatment of fevers to indigestion to back pains to toothaches. These remedies were a part of a woman's everyday life and were never considered for patenting, though later on, modern medicine and pharmaceuticals, after careful analysis of their curative properties, developed these same remedies and patented them so they could sell them in drugstores. In fact, not many people realize that a variety of instruments in the medical field were invented and patented by women—stretchers, splints, field ambulances, to name a few.

In the field of science, women who were distinguished enough to merit working alongside men have been few and far between. These women, out of sheer determination, helped pave the way for other women to follow in their footsteps. Today, female researchers and scholars continuously delve into the past to find the untold half of history—the half which tells the story of women made invisible by patriarchal societies. We now know that hundreds of women were the inventors of hundreds of items that are taken for granted in today's world—from engineering to computers to astronomy to mathematics and more. As more women became educated in these traditionally male fields, more women were employed by large corporations and, in the last twenty-five years, almost half of all the patents granted to women pertain to chemical technology.

Today, the use of computers is an integral part of our lives and, as a result, an unprecedented number of women are entering the field of IT. However, women have always played an important role from the earliest days of computing. Ada Lovelace was a brilliant mathematician who, with her friend and mentor Charles Babbage, conceived of an analytical machine or engine that could handle symbols, letters, and numbers in such a way to code and decode information through a series of repeated instructions. This method of codification was stored on punch cards, which were used in early computers. This process of coding and decoding is what is known today as looping and is what many computer programs still use. In 1980, the United States Department of Defense used many of her theories to create a computer language, MIL-STD-1815, which they called Ada in her honor.

Other women who have contributed to the field of computers are Grace Murray Hopper (later promoted to Rear Admiral) who distinguished herself as a programmer and helped in the development of two widely used computer languages, FORTRAN and COBOL; and Betty Holberton, better known for her work in human engineering or the user-friendliness of languages and systems. She initiated the standard numeric pad in the keyboard. Thanks to women in the field, the keyboard layout is what it is today, as are the colors that help make working on a computer less wearisome to the eyes.

Though the number of female students in engineering and IT courses has slowly declined since their peak in the late 1980s, women are still earning bachelor's degrees in the field. The steady decline is said to be due to the misconceptions and stereotypes surrounding the computer world such as the geek factor which typifies the computer techie in a dirty and overly cluttered basement, tinkering with a host of different gadgets.

In an attempt at luring women back into the field, educational programs have tried to make computer science more appealing to women by keeping software packages to a minimum and allowing for as much pure logic as possible. Large companies like IBM offer camps for young girls in the fields of mathematics, science, and engineering. The camp, aptly called EX.I.T.E. (Exploring Interests in Technology and Engineering), provides hands-on learning while, at the same time, developing, from an early age, a liking to these traditionally male fields. Aside from these camps, IBM also hosts events and conferences, such as the Grace Hopper Celebration of Women, which allow women to present their work, share ideas, and collaborate with each other.

Other groups and organizations that cater to women in technology are: National Center for Women and Information Technology (NCWIT), Association for Progressive Communications, Women's Networking Support Programme, Association for Women in Computing, LinuxChix, and others.

Feminism has also made it possible for courses and educational programs to gear IT toward women. All over the world are outreach programs that provide mentoring, scholarships, and opportunities to women in schools and colleges; some programs target disadvantaged girls, some target women in developing countries. One such program is Feminist Approach to Technology (FAT) in India where back in the 1960s enrollment of women in engineering was less than one percent. By 2007, it had risen to approximately sixteen percent. Their mission is to give women a chance at participating in technology by increasing their awareness of it and debunking the age-long myth that women do poorly in science fields. Not only does FAT aid in skill building, it also gives technical assistance to already established women's organizations, which may need support in order to achieve their own goals. Aside from this, FAT brings together women in technology within workshops and seminars where they share ideas and teach new techniques that provide women with a system of support and interaction.

CONCLUDING REMARKS

Feminism is a philosophy that values women as a whole. It is not a war against men, and it definitely is not a war to try to impose a matriarchal system that oppresses men. On the contrary. Feminism is a philosophy that tries to dismantle the unfair and misogynistic attitudes of a patriarchal society toward one half of its population: women.

Feminism believes in equality because feminism is based on the social, economic, and political equality of men and women; and together with this equality comes the responsibility of women to define their role as individuals in such areas as profession, career, marriage, and motherhood—areas that have, thus far, been socially validated for women as the expected roles of womanhood.

A feminist can be anybody: woman or man, old or young. Therefore, not all feminists are women. However, because many feminists are women, many people (both men and women) believe the matter to be a battle of the sexes, or a man vs. woman issue. It is not. Worse, social values have made feminism into an ideology of hatred against men which is unfortunate since this rift ultimately masks the reality of a continued violation of human rights. In short, all feminists are asking for is to be recognized as a human being, not inferior, not second rate, and not subordinate to men.

Not all women are feminists, and as such, they go contrary to the feminist belief in equality. Feminism believes in equality of the sexes—after all, both men and women are part of the same race. Sadly, religion, cultural values, traditions, and prejudice (especially chauvinism) have contributed to the manipulation of the minds of many women (and men) into believing and accepting a patriarchal system where men are deemed to be superior and women inferior.

It is because of the above that, sometimes, it is very difficult to talk about feminism dispassionately because it has been made into a controversial topic in our society. By definition, feminism is related to emotions because feminism is about a woman's life and her personal growth; and historically speaking, a woman has never been a person in her own right. A woman, even to this date in many societies, is still considered the daughter of a man, the wife of a man, and the mother of boy. It is little wonder that feminism has no other choice but to be an emotionally charged issue. In fact, anger made the first wave of feminists stand up and speak for themselves and for others when the injustices were no longer tolerable. Anger was the backbone of caucuses, coalitions, organizations, and groups that empowered and inspired the women of the second wave of feminists; and anger still continues to be the driving force of the next generation of women that continue to follow in their mothers' footsteps in trying to stamp out the injustices committed daily against women for the mere fact that they were born female.

Whether the feminist movement is divided into waves or not, the reality is that there is a strong women's movement that has opened dialogues for women and has gained support and given strength to many women in a common attempt at deconstructing the patriarchal stereotype of what a woman should, could, and must be.

It is because of these stereotypes that, during the course of the women's movement, women have branched out into different interests and subgroups dealing with a wide variety of issues, from the right to vote to abolition to temperance to pornography to family values to LGBT issues to education to job security to child abuse . . . with a thousand other topics in between—topics that, for the most part, make up the fabric of society, but are of no direct concern to the patriarchal system.

Whether women wish to stay at home and raise a family or go to work and earn a second income is (in many cases) a choice that the woman of today can now make. It is a choice that a more open society has given her, and it is a choice that she can take without the repercussions of ostracism or criticism.

What is of great value is that the persistent anger and determination of feminism has created a society that, for the most part, has become more accepting of alternative choices for women. Women no longer have to stay at home to raise a family. They can choose their jobs or professions regardless of whether their husbands, fathers, or other male figures agree or disagree. In other words, thanks to feminism, the power structure has shifted slightly, and men have been thrown into the equation for a reevaluation of their roles alongside those of women. Though the ideal situation of a society where men and women have exactly the same rights is still far away, the women's movement will continue to strive for a balanced world.

Still, as the world changes attitudes and values, educational programs, politics, and other areas of society also change their points of view to embrace women issues that will allow for women's studies, feminist research, and a women's political agenda that will enable identification, isolation, and a positive solution to the new social issues that arise.

Because of this, feminism will forever continue to face and confront new challenges in their never ending quest for true equality.

Appendices

APPENDIX I

THE SENECA FALLS DECLARATION (1848)
Elizabeth Cady Stanton

Declaration of Sentiments

When, in the course of human events, it becomes necessary for one portion of the family of man to assume among the people of the earth a position different from that which they have hitherto occupied, but one to which the laws of nature and of nature's God entitle them, a decent respect to the opinions of mankind requires that they should declare the causes that impel them to such a course.

We hold these truths to be self-evident: that all men and women are created equal; that they are endowed by their Creator with certain inalienable rights; that among these are life, liberty, and the pursuit of happiness; that to secure these rights governments are instituted, deriving their just powers from the consent of the governed. Whenever any form of government becomes destructive of these ends, it is the right of those who suffer from it to refuse allegiance to it, and to insist upon the institution of a new government, laying its foundation on such principles, and organizing its powers in such form, as to them shall seem most likely to affect their safety and happiness. Prudence, indeed, will dictate that governments long established should not be changed for light and transient causes; and accordingly all experience hath shown that mankind are more disposed to suffer, while evils are sufferable, than to right themselves by abolishing the forms to which they are accustomed. But when a long train of abuses and usurpations, pursuing invariably the same object, evinces a design to reduce them under absolute despotism, it is their duty to throw off such government, and to provide new guards for their future security. Such has been the patient sufferance of the women under this government, and such is now the necessity which constrains them to demand the equal station to which they are entitled. The history of mankind is a history of repeated injuries and usurpations on the part of man toward woman, having in direct object the establishment of an absolute tyranny over her. To prove this, let facts be submitted to a candid world.

He has never permitted her to exercise her inalienable right to the elective franchise.

He has compelled her to submit to laws, in the formation of which she had no voice.

He has withheld from her rights which are given to the most ignorant and degraded men—both natives and foreigners.

Having deprived her of this first right of a citizen, the elective franchise, thereby leaving her without representation in the halls of legislation, he has oppressed her on all sides.

He has made her, if married, in the eye of the law, civilly dead.

He has taken from her all right in property, even to the wages she earns.

He has made her, morally, an irresponsible being,

as she can commit many crimes with impunity, provided they be done in the presence of her husband. In the covenant of marriage, she is compelled to promise obedience to her husband, he becoming, to all intents and purposes, her master—the law giving him power to deprive her of her liberty, and to administer chastisement.

He has so framed the laws of divorce, as to what shall be the proper causes, and in case of separation, to whom the guardianship of the children shall be given, as to be wholly regardless of the happiness of women—the law, in all cases, going upon a false supposition of the supremacy of man, and giving all power into his hands.

After depriving her of all rights as a married woman, if single, and the owner of property, he has taxed her to support a government which recognizes her only when her property can be made profitable to it.

He has monopolized nearly all the profitable employments, and from those she is permitted to follow, she receives but a scanty remuneration. He closes against her all the avenues to wealth and distinction which he considers most honorable to himself. As a teacher of theology, medicine, or law, she is not known.

He has denied her the facilities for obtaining a thorough education, all colleges being closed against her.

He allows her in church, as well as state, but a subordinate position, claiming apostolic authority for her exclusion from the ministry, and, with some exceptions, from any public participation in the affairs of the church.

He has created a false public sentiment by giving to the world a different code of morals for men and women, by which moral delinquencies which exclude women from society, are not only tolerated, but deemed of little account in man.

He has usurped the prerogative of Jehovah himself, claiming it as his right to assign for her a sphere of action, when that belongs to her conscience and to her God.

He has endeavored, in every way that he could, to destroy her confidence in her own powers, to lessen her self-respect, and to make her willing to lead a dependent and abject life.

Now, in view of this entire disfranchisement of one-half the people of this country, their social and religious degradation—in view of the unjust laws above mentioned, and because women do feel themselves aggrieved, oppressed, and fraudulently deprived of their most sacred rights, we insist that they have immediate admission to all the rights and privileges which belong to them as citizens of the United States.

In entering upon the great work before us, we anticipate no small amount of misconception, misrepresentation, and ridicule; but we shall use every instrumentality within our power to effect our object. We shall employ agents, circulate tracts, petition the State and national Legislatures, and endeavor to enlist the pulpit and the press in our behalf. We hope this Convention will be followed by a series of Conventions, embracing every part of the country.

APPENDIX 2

The following are short biographies of notable characters.

Sappho

Was born sometime between 630 and 612 B.C. She was born of an aristocratic family in the Isle of Lesbos, and because of her family's position she was able to choose whatever she wanted to do in life. She chose to study the arts, music, and poetry. Although she traveled around Greece, she spent most of her time on Lesbos. She excelled at poetry, refining the existing lyric meter to such a precise point that today it carries her name: Sapphic meter.

Sappho is most well known for her poetry. Her poetry is the only documentation we have nowadays that affords us an insight into the Greece of that era. Most of her works have unfortunately been lost. Only one exists in its entirety, "Hymn to Aphrodite," but we have several fragments of others that allow us to rejoice in her cries of love, passion, anguish, and longing. These human experiences and emotions are the basis of her works. Most of these poems were written as a tribute to women, and specifically to Aphrodite, Goddess of Love.

Sappho is considered the tenth Muse for her contributions to music and poetry, although she is also noted for her work as teacher/mentor/guide in a school/aesthetic club for young girls where she taught them arts, music, and poetry as well as teaching them to pay tribute to goddesses. The girls also learned about human experiences and emotions.

Much has been speculated about Sappho. She is, and will continue to be, an enigma because history has made sure that only a glimpse of her remains. Her works have been translated from her native dialect, and many translations conflict. Fanciful writers have created a Sappho totally engrossed in female love, when in fact, Sappho enjoyed equally the company of men and women. In fact, she was married and had a daughter by the name of Cleis. Other even more romantic writers speak of one Sappho, perhaps a second Sappho, that fell in love with Phaon, a hero, a beautiful sailor, insensitive to love, who was endowed by Aphrodite with virility and youth, and with a gift of having all women fall in love with him and, because of his rejection of Sappho's advances, Sappho threw herself in despair from the cliff of Leucus.

Whatever the reality and whatever the myth, Sappho remains as the great poetess and the woman whose name is synonymous with homosexual love between women: Sapphic and Lesbian.

Sojourner Truth

Sojourner Truth was born in 1797 as Isabella Baumfree. She was one of thirteen slave children born to slave parents in upstate New York. Because the area was a Dutch settlement at the time, Isabella first learned to speak Dutch and later, when sold as a slave at the age of eleven, was forced to learn English under the cruel treatment of her new master. She was sold twice more before finally ending up with her third master, John Dumont. It was here that she met and married another slave, Thomas, and with whom she had five children. When campaigning started for abolition, Dumont promised Isabella freedom, but reneged on his promise, and Isabella ran away with her infant son. Soon after, the State of New York granted freedom to slaves. She was legally a free woman.

One legacy her mother had left Isabella was a deep sense of Christian faith. When Isabella, then a free woman, settled in New York City, she worked as domestic help in religious communes. While there, she discovered that a member of the Dumont family had sold one of her children in Alabama (a state that had not yet passed laws to free slaves), and since this son had been legally emancipated under New York Law, Isabella sued the Dumont family member and won the case, thus winning her son's return to freedom.

In 1843, Isabella had a spiritual revelation that led her to change her name and change her life. She believed this revelation came from the Holy Spirit and that her mission in life was to be a traveling preacher. She chose the name Sojourner Truth for that purpose. She traveled through Long Island, Connecticut, and finally Northampton, Massachussetts, preaching God's truth and salvation. She met and worked with such abolitionists as William Lloyd Garrison and Frederick Douglass.

During the Civil War, Sojourner Truth raised food and clothing contributions for black regiments and, in 1864, she tried to challenge discrimination by race in segregated street cars in Washington D.C.

Being a woman, she realized the need for rights, so she added woman's suffrage to her agenda and spoke of her personal life as both slave and woman. In 1851, she spoke at the Women's Convention in Akron, Ohio, where she gave her legendary speech, "Ain't I a Woman."

Sojourner Truth continued to preach and lecture until her death in 1883.

Rosa Parks

Rosa Parks, with her courage, determination, and dignity is, without a doubt, the mother of the modern day civil rights movement. Her courageous act of defiance against a segregated system triggered a wave of protests that marked history, redirecting it into its present course.

Rosa Louise McCauley was born on February 4, 1913 in Tuskegee, Alabama. She was educated in the local rural school and went to Alabama State Teacher's College High School. Due to the illness (and subsequent death) of, first, her grandmother and, later on, her mother, Rosa left school to take care of them, delaying her high school studies. She did not receive her high school diploma until she was in her twenties.

Rosa married Raymond Parks, an activist, and together with him, worked in the National Association for the Advancement of Colored People (NAACP) programs. Though she volunteered her time there as a secretary for the Montgomery Chapter, she held a full time job as seamstress at the Montgomery Fair department store.

One fateful day, after a full day at work, Rosa

boarded the bus and sat down. A sign separated the white section from the colored section; but the driver reserved the right to move the sign if there were many whites standing. At the time of boarding the bus, Rosa Parks sat in the colored section. But as the bus filled up with white people, the driver decided to move the sign back. When he asked Rosa and three other black passengers to give up their seats, Rosa refused. She was arrested.

After her arrest, other minority groups, the African-American community of Montgomery, and sympathizers of struggles of African-Americans, led by Dr. Martin Luther King, Jr., organized and promoted a boycott of the city buses that lasted over a year. Thousands across the nation joined in sit-ins, eat-ins, and marches. Though there were waves of retaliation where black churches were burned, and even Dr. King's home was bombed, the community stood firm.

Rosa Parks' arrest was not the actual cause of the Montgomery boycott; it was, however, a precipitating factor long overdue. The black community had suffered similar degrading treatments in the hands of white bus drivers for a long time. The Montgomery bus boycott will be remembered as the largest and most successful mass movements against racial segregation in history. It helped spark many other protests, and it catapulted Dr. King to the forefront of the Civil Rights Movement.

Mrs. Parks has been a role model for youths. Mrs. Parks received more than forty-three honorary doctorate degrees, and thousands of certificates, medals, plaques, and awards. She is the first living person to be honored with a public holiday. The first

Monday following February 4th is Mrs. Parks Day in the state of Michigan, her home state. Mrs. Rosa Parks died peacefully on October 24, 2005.

APPENDIX 3

Notable Women Philosophers

Hypatia of Alexandria, (370-415)
Mary Astell, (1666-1731)
Teresa of Avila, (1515-1582)
Hildegard of Bingen, (1098-1179)
Elisabeth of Bohemia, (1618-1680)
Mary Whiton Calkins, (1863-1930)
Margaret Cavendish, (1623-1673)
Émilie du Châtelet, (1706-1749)
Catherine Trotter Cockburn, (1679-1749)
Lady Anne Finch Conway, (1631-1679)
George Eliot, (1819-1880)
Charlotte Perkins Gilman, (1860-1935)
Hipparchia, (4th century BC)
Susanne Langer, (1895-1985)

Rosa Luxemburg, (1871-1919)
Harriet Martineau, (1802-1876)
Damaris Cudworth Masham, (1659-1708)
Harriet Taylor Mill, (1807-1858)
Christine de Pizan, (c. 1365-c. 1430)
Anna Maria van Schurman, (1607-1678)
Lady Mary Shepherd, (1777-1847)
Anne Louise Germaine de Staël, (1766-1817)
L. Susan Stebbing, (1885-1943)
Gabrielle Suchon, (1631-1703)
Victoria, Lady Welby, (1837-1912)
Mary Wollstonecraft, (1759-1797)
Dorothy Maud Wrinch, (1894-1976)

Political Campaigns

Anti-Slavery Society
Woman Suffrage
Prohibition
Child Labour

Journals and Magazines

Women's Journal
Woman Voter
Woman Citizen
The Suffragist

Campaigning Organizations

American Woman Suffrage Association
National Association of Colored Women
National Consumers League
Woman's Peace Party
National Woman Suffrage Association
National American Woman Suffrage Association
Congressional Union for Woman Suffrage
League of Women Voters
Woman's Trade Union League

Male Supporters of Women Suffrage

Clarence Batchelor
Charles Beard
John Bengough
Eugene V. Debs
Floyd Dell
Frederick Douglass
William DuBois
Max Eastman
Daniel Fitzpatrick
George W. Julian
Paul Kellogg

Rollin Kirby
Samuel J. May
Robert Minor
John Reed
Boardman Robinson
Charles Edward Russell
Upton Sinclair
John Sloan
Norman Thomas
Benjamin Wade
Art Young

Campaigners for Women's Rights

Edith Abbott
Grace Abbott
Jane Addams
Susan Anthony
Emily Balch
Mary Ritter Beard
Emily Blackwell
Elizabeth Blackwell
Amelia Bloomer
Ella Bloor

Nellie Bly
Madeline Breckinridge
Sophonisba Breckinridge
Olympia Brown
Pearl Buck
Lucy Burns
Mary Ann Cary
Carrie Chapman Catt
Maria Weston Chapman
Lydia Maria Child

Dorothy Day
Rheta Childe Dorr
Crystal Eastman
Elizabeth Flynn
Margaret Fuller
Mathilda Joslyn Gage
Charlotte PerkinsGilman
Mabel Gillespie
Susan Glaspell
Emma Goldman
Josephine Goldmark
Angelina Grimke
Sarah Grimke
Sarah Hale
Margaret Haley
Alice Hamilton
Ida H. Harper
Frances Harper
Josephine Herbst
Juliet Ward Howe
Mary 'Mother' Jones
Helen Keller
Florence Kelley
Mary Kenney
Freda Kirchwey
Belle LaFollette
Julia Lathrop
Mary Lease
Lena Morrow Lewis
Mary Livermore
Belva Ann Lockwood
Adella Logan
Mabel Dodge Luman
Mary Mahoney
Helen Marot
Katharine McCormick
Mary McDowell
Inez Milholland
Adena Miller
Lucretia Mott
Agnes Nestor
Kate Richards O'Hare
Leonora O'Reilly

Mary Kenney O'Sullivan
Mary White Ovington
Maud Park
Elsie Clews Parsons
Lucy Parsons
Alice Paul
Francis Perkins
Jeanette Rankin
Margaret Robins
Edith Nourse Rogers
Eleanor Roosevelt
Josephine Ruffin
Margaret Sanger
Rosie Scheiderman
Rosika Schwimmer
Anna Howard Shaw
Agnes Smedley
Ida Wise Smith
Mary J. Stafford
Elizabeth Cady Stanton
Ellen Gates Starr
Doris Stevens
Alzina Stevens
Rosa Pastor Stokes
Lucy Stone
Jane Swisshelm
Mary B. Talbert
Ida Tarbell
Mary Church Terrell
Dorothy Thompson
Sojourner Truth
Mabel Vernon
Fanny Garrison Villard
Mary Heaton Vorse
Lillian Wald
Mary Walker
Olivia Washington
Ida Wells
Anne Whitney
Frances Willard
Victoria Woodhull
Fanny Wright

APPENDIX 4

Married Women's Property Act

Passed April 7, 1848. The People of the State of New York, represented in Senate and Assembly do enact as follows:

- Sec. 1. The real and personal property of any female who may hereafter marry, and which she shall own at the time of marriage, and the rents issues and profits thereof shall not be subject to the disposal of her husband, nor be liable for his debts, and shall continue her sole and separate property, as if she were a single female.
- Sec. 2 The real and personal property, and the rents issues and profits thereof of any female now married shall not be subject to the disposal of her husband; but shall be her sole and separate property as if she were a single female except so far as the same may be liable for the debts of her husband heretofore contracted.
- Sec. 3. It shall be lawful for any married female to receive, by gift, grant devise or bequest, from any person other than her husband and hold to her sole and separate use, as if she were a single female, real and personal property, and the rents, issues and profits thereof, and the same shall not be subject to the disposal of her husband, nor be liable for his debts.
- Sec. 4. All contracts made between persons in contemplation of marriage shall remain in full force after such marriage takes place.

APPENDIX 5

Ain't I a Woman
Women's Convention in Akron, Ohio, 1851

Well, children, where there is so much racket there must be something out of kilter. I think that 'twixt the Negroes of the South and the women at the North, all talking about rights, the white men will be in a fix pretty soon. But what's all this here talking about?

That man over there says that women need to be helped into carriages, and lifted over ditches, and to have the best place everywhere. Nobody ever helps me into carriages, or over mud-puddles, or gives me any best place! And ain't I a woman? Look at me! Look at my arm! I have ploughed and planted, and gathered into barns, and no man could head me! And ain't I a woman? I could work as much and eat as much as a man—when I could get it—and bear the lash as well! And ain't I a woman? I have borne thirteen children, and seen most all sold off to slavery, and when I cried out with my mother's grief, none but Jesus heard me! And ain't I a woman?

Then they talk about this thing in the head; what's this they call it? [member of audience whispers, "intellect"] That's it, honey. What's that got to do with women's rights or Negroes' rights? If my cup won't hold but a pint, and yours holds a quart, wouldn't you be mean not to let me have my little half measure full?

Then that little man in black there, he says women can't have as much rights as men, 'cause Christ wasn't a woman! Where did your Christ come from? Where did your Christ come from? From God and a woman! Man had nothing to do with Him.

If the first woman God ever made was strong enough to turn the world upside down all alone, these women together ought to be able to turn it back, and get it right side up again! And now they is asking to do it, the men better let them.

Obliged to you for hearing me, and now old Sojourner ain't got nothing more to say.

APPENDIX 6

Jim Crow Laws

as compiled by the Martin Luther King, Jr., National Historic Site Interpretive Staff. (This is a partial list derived from a larger compilation composed by the Martin Luther King, Jr., National Historic Site Interpretive Staff. From: http//www.nps.gov/malu/documents/jim crowlaws.htm.)

- Barbers. No colored barber shall serve as a barber (to) white girls or women (Georgia).
- Blind Wards. The board of trustees shall . . . maintain a separate building...on separate ground for the admission, care, instruction, and support of all blind persons of the colored or Black race (Louisiana).
- Burial. The officer in charge shall not bury, or allow to be buried, any colored persons upon ground set apart or used for the burial of white persons (Georgia).
- Buses. All passenger stations in this state operated by any motor transportation company shall have separate waiting rooms or space and separate ticket windows for the white and colored races (Alabama).
- Child Custody. It shall be unlawful for any parent, relative, or other white person in this State, having the control or custody of any white child, by right of guardianship, natural or acquired, or otherwise, to dispose of, give or surrender such white child permanently into the custody, control, maintenance, or support, of a Negro (South Carolina).
- Education. The schools for white children and the schools for Negro children shall be conducted separately (Florida).

- Libraries. The state librarian is directed to fit up and maintain a separate place for the use of the colored people who may come to the library for the purpose of reading books or periodicals (North Carolina).
- Mental Hospitals. The Board of Control shall see that proper and distinct apartments are arranged for said patients, so that in no case shall Negroes and white persons be together (Georgia).
- Militia. The white and colored militia shall be separately enrolled, and shall never be compelled to serve in the same organization. No organization of colored troops shall be permitted where white troops are available and where whites are permitted to be organized, colored troops shall be under the command of white officers (North Carolina).
- Nurses. No person or corporation shall require any white female nurse to nurse in wards or rooms in hospitals, either public or private, in which Negro men are placed (Alabama).
- Prisons. The warden shall see that the white convicts shall have separate apartments for both eating and sleeping from the Negro convicts (Mississippi).
- Reform Schools. The children of white and colored races committed to the houses of reform shall be kept entirely separate from each other (Kentucky).
- Teaching. Any instructor who shall teach in any school, college or institution where members of the white and colored race are received and enrolled as pupils for instruction shall be deemed guilty of a misdemeanor, and upon conviction thereof, shall be fined . . . (Oklahoma).
- Wine and Beer. All persons licensed to conduct the business of selling beer or wine...shall serve either white people exclusively or colored people exclusively and shall not sell to the two races within the same room at any time (Georgia).

BIBLIOGRAPHY

Abbott, Margaret Post, Mary Ellen Chijioke, Pink Dandelion, and John W. Oliver Jr. *Historical Dictionary of the Friends*. Lanham, Md. : Scarecrow Press, 2003.

Adam, Barry. *The Rise of a Gay and Lesbian Movement*. Boston: Twayne Publishers, 1987.

Archer, Jules. *Breaking Barriers: the Feminist Revolution, from Susan B. Anthony to Margaret Sanger to Betty Friedan*. New York, N.Y.: Viking, 1991.

Bacon, Margaret Hope. *Mothers of feminism: The Story of Quaker Women in America*. San Francisco: Harper & Row, 1986.

Baker, Jean H. *Sisters: The Lives of America's Suffragists*. New York: Hill and Wang, 2005.

Baumgardner, Jennifer. *Abortion & Life*. New York: Akashic Books, 2008.

Beadie, Nancy and Kim Tolley, eds. *Chartered Schools: Two Hundred Years of Independent Academies in the United States, 1727-1925*. Studies in the History of Education. New York: RoutledgeFalmer, 2002.

Bernard, Jacqueline. *Journey Toward Freedom: The Story of Sojourner Truth*. New York: The Feminist Press at CUNY, 1993.

Boles, Janet K. and Diane Long Hoeveler, eds. *From the Goddess to the Glass Ceiling: a Dictionary of Feminism*. Lanham, Md.: Madison Books, 1996.

Booth, Catherine Mumford. *Female Ministry: Or Woman's Right to Preach the Gospel*. New York : Salvation Army Supplies, Print. and Pub. Dept., 1975.

Colman, Penny. *Rosie the Riveter: Women Working On The Home Front in World War II*. New York: Crown Publishers, 1995.

Dœuff, Michèle Le. *Hipparchia's Choice: An Essay Concerning Women, Philosophy, Etc.* Translated by Trista Selous. Oxford, UK ; Cambridge, MA: Blackwell, 1991.

Dupré, Louis. *The Enlightenment and the Intellectual Foundations of Modern Culture.* New Haven: Yale University Press, 2004.

Durán, María Ángeles. *El Ama de Casa: Crítica Política de la Economía Doméstica.* Lee y discute, 87. Bilbao: Zero, 1978.

Edsall, Nicholas. *Toward Stonewall: Homosexuality and Society in the Modern Western World.* Charlottesville Va.: University of Virginia Press, 2003.

Evans, Judith. *Feminist Theory Today: An Introduction to Second-Wave Feminism.* London; Thousand Oaks, Calif.: Sage Publications, 1995.

Evans, Richard J. *The Feminists: Women's Emancipation Movements In Europe, America, And Australasia, 1840-1920.* London: Croom Helm; New York: Barnes & Noble Books, 1977.

Fox, George. *The Journal of George Fox.* Edited by Norman Penney. New York: Cosimo Classics, 2007.

Freedman, Estelle B. *No Turning Back: The History of Feminism and the Future of Women.* New York: Ballantine Books, 2003.

Gilbert, H. Barnes and Dwight L. Dumond, eds. "Theodore Weld to Sarah and Angelina Grimké, August 15, 1837" published in *The Letters of Theodore Weld, Angelina Grimké Weld and Sarah M. Grimké, 1822-1844, Vol. I.* New York: Da Capo Press, 1970. p. 425-432.

Gillis, Stacy, Gillian Howie and Rebecca Munford, eds. *Third Wave Feminism: A Critical Exploration.* Basingstoke: Palgrave Macmillan, 2007.

Grimke, Sarah Moore. *Letters On The Equality Of The Sexes And The Condition Of Woman: Addressed To Mary S. Parker, President Of The Boston Female Anti-Slavery Society.* Whitefish, Montana: Kessinger Publishing, 2007.

Greer, Germaine. *The Whole Woman.* New York: A.A. Knopf, 1999.

Hawken, Paul. *Blessed Unrest: How the Largest Movement in the World Came Into Being, and Why No One Saw it Coming.* New York: Viking, 2007.

Henry, Astrid. *Not My Mother's Sister: Generational Conflict and Third-Wave Feminism.* Bloomington: Indiana University Press, 2004.

Hill, Jonathan. *Faith in the Age of Reason: The Enlightenment from Galileo to Kant.* Downers Grove, Ill.: InterVarsity Press, 2004.

Hoffert, Sylvia D. *When Hens Crow: The Woman's Right Movement in Antebellum America.* Bloomington: Indiana University Press, 1995.

Hoff-Wilson, Joan. *Law, Gender, and Injustice: A Legal History of U.S. Women.* New York: New York University Press, 1991.

Jacob, Margaret. *Enlightenment: A Brief History with Documents.* Boston: Bedford/St. Martin's, 2001.

Johnson, Merri Lisa, ed. *Jane Sexes It Up: True Confessions of Feminist Desire.* New York: Four Walls Eight Windows, 2002.

Kirkland, Caroline Matilda. *Holidays Abroad: Europe from the West. Vols. 1 and 2.* Charleston, S.C.: Nabu Press, 2010.

Kramarae, Cheris, and Paula A. Treichler. *A Feminist Dictionary.* London; Boston: Pandora Press, 1985.

Mabee, Carleton. *Sojourner Truth: Slave, Prophet, Legend.* New York: New York University Press, 1995.

Macdonald, Fiona. *Women in 19th-century America.* New York: Peter Bedrick Books, 1999.

Maynard, Mary, and June Purvis, eds. *New Frontiers in Women's Studies: Knowledge, Identity and Nationalism.* London; Bristol, PA: Taylor & Francis, 1996.

McFadden, Margaret H. *Golden Cables of Sympathy : The Transatlantic Sources of Nineteenth-Century Feminism.* Lexington, Ky. : University Press of Kentucky, 1999.

Paulson, Ross Evans. *Liberty, Equality and Justice: Civil Rights, Women's Rights, and the Regulation of Business, 1865-1932.* Durham, NC: Duke University Press, 1997.

Payment, Simone. *Queen Latifah*. New York: Rosen Pub. Group, 2006.

Peterson, Susan Louise. *The Changing Meaning of Feminism: Life Cycle and Career Implications from a Sociological Perspective*. San Francisco : International Scholars Publications, 1998.

Porter, Roy. *The Enlightenment*. Houndmills, Basingstoke, Hampshire; New York: Palgrave, 2001.

Punshon, John. *Portrait in Grey: A Short History of the Quakers*. London: Quaker Home Service, 1984.

Redding, Saunders. "Sojourner Truth" in *Notable American Women 1607-1950, Volume III P-Z*. Edited by Edward T. James. Cambridge, Mass.: Belknap Press of Harvard University Press, 1971.

Rich, Adrianne. "Disobedience is what NWSA is Potentially About." *Women's Studies Quarterly* 9, no. 3 (1981): 4-5.

Robinson, Victoria, and Diane Richardson, eds. *Introducing Women's Studies: Feminist Theory and Practice*. Washington Square, N.Y.: New York University, 1997.

Russell, Diana E. H. *Rape in marriage*. Bloomington, Ind. : Indiana University Press, 1990.

Sabrosky, Judith A,. *From Rationality to Liberation : The Evolution of Feminist Ideology*. Westport, Conn.: Greenwood Press, 1979.

Salmon, Marylynn. *Women and the Law of Property in Early America*. Chapel Hill : University of North Carolina Press, 1986.

Snyder, Jane McIntosh. *Lesbian Desire in The Lyrics of Sappho*. New York : Columbia University Press, 1997.

Stein, Marc, ed. "Pride Marches and Parades" in *Encyclopedia of Lesbian, Gay, Bisexual, and Transgender History in America*. New York, NY : Charles Scribner's Sons/Thomson/ Gale, 2004.

Stetson, Erlene and Linda David. *Glorying in Tribulation: The Lifework of Sojourner Truth*. East Lansing : Michigan State University Press, 1994.

Tate, Eleanora E. *African American Musicians (Black Stars)*. New York: Wiley and Sons Inc., 2000.

Tolley. Kim. *The Science Education of American Girls: A Historical Perspective*. New York : RoutledgeFalmer, 2003.

Tong, Rosemarie8. *Feminist Thought: A More Comprehensive Introduction*. Boulder, Colo. : Westview Press, 2009.

Tristan, Flora. *The London journal of Flora Tristan, 1842, or, The aristocracy and the working class of England*. Translated and edited by Jean Hawkes. London: Virago, 1982.

Walker, Rebecca. "Becoming the Third Wave" in *Ms. Magazine* (January/February, 1992): 39–41.

Warnock, Mary, ed. *Women Philosophers*. London: J.M. Dent, 1996.

Wolf, Naomi. *The Beauty Myth: How Images of Beauty are Used Against Women*. New York: Perennial, 2002.

About the Author

Born in Venezuela of Spanish and Venezuelan parents, Maria M. Bermudez was raised in Europe where she completed a BSc in Psychology and a MA in Anthropology from the University of London. In 2003, she obtained a Masters in Liberal Studies in Women's Studies from Eastern Michigan University (USA) and, upon completion, she stayed on at Eastern to lecture her own-designed course: "Introduction to Women in Latin America." She has been in the teaching field for over twenty years, and her passion for travel and seeing different cultures has taken her to many countries across three continents: Africa, North and South America, and Europe.

She currently lives in Canada where she lectures at the University of Windsor.

CPSIA information can be obtained at www.ICGtesting.com
Printed in the USA
BVOW04s1902191214

380210BV00009B/48/P